THE TAO OF CONFIDENCE

Mastering the Inner Game of Life

Aery Prabhakar

UNICORN BOOKS

Publishers
UNICORN BOOKS
F-2/16, Ansari Road, Daryaganj, New Delhi-110002
☎ 23275434, 23262683, 23262783 • Fax: 011-23257790
E-mail: info@unicornbooks.in • *Website:* www.unicornbooks.in

Distributors
Pustak Mahal®
J-3/16, Daryaganj, New Delhi-110002
☎ 23276539, 23272783, 23272784 • Fax: 011-23260518
E-mail: info@pustakmahal.com • *Website:* www.pustakmahal.com

Sales Centres

- 10-B, Netaji Subhash Marg, Daryaganj, New Delhi-110002
  ☎ 23268292, 23268293, 23279900 • Fax: 011-23280567
  E-mail: salespmahal@airtelmail.in
  rapidexdelhi@indiatimes.com
- 6686, Khari Baoli, Delhi-110006
  ☎ 23944314, 23911979
- ***Bengaluru:*** ☎ 080-22234025 • Telefax: 080-22240209
  E-mail: pustak@airtelmail.in • pustak@sancharnet.in
- ***Mumbai:*** ☎ 022-22010941, 022-22053387
  E-mail: rapidex@bom5.vsnl.net.in
- ***Patna:*** ☎ 0612-3294193 • Telefax: 0612-2302719
  E-mail: rapidexptn@rediffmail.com
- ***Hyderabad:*** Telefax: 040-24737290
  E-mail: pustakmahalhyd@yahoo.co.in

ISBN: 978-81-7806-183-2

Edition : January, 2010

Printed at : Param Offsetters, Okhla, New Delhi-110020

To those men and women around the world,
who have unshakeable confidence, and
who wouldn't settle for anything less than
their deepest dreams

To my parents, whose love and trust
instilled tremendous strength in me
and made me believe that I CAN!

Legal Notice

The information in this book includes mention of sex, sexual practices and sexual behaviours which are of course, discussed only where they are relevant to the subject of the book. If you are offended in any way by this kind of discussion, please do NOT read any further.

If however, you are ready to change your life and breathe in your new-found world of total, unstoppable self-confidence, then read on…!

Contents

Acknowledgement

My heartiest thanks go to everyone who has helped me to walk upon the path of helping others recognising their true inner potential.

To **Anthony Robbins**, **Brian Tracy**, **David De Angelo**, **Kenrick Cleveland**, **Kevin Hogan**, **Derek Vitalio** and **Dr. Wayne Dyer** who have been key to my turning towards this amazing field of personal development.

To **Marie Forleo** who kicked me into action when my dreams were just dreams and gave me a kick-start towards making them a reality.

To **Late Mr. Napoleon Hill**, whose book ***The Law of Success*** gave me tremendous hope and courage in the most trying period of my life, and connected me to my innermost purpose.

To my **Parents**, whose sacrifice and perspiration to make me what I am today is worth more than anything I can ever return.

I would like to thank **Mr. Rajesh Jaitley**, whose brotherly love, guidance and an unshakeable belief in me has always been an infinite source of inspiration and the force behind all my efforts, including this book.

Preface

By the time you finish reading this book, you will have mastered the ultimate secrets of developing an unshakeable self-confidence.

As you read this book, you'll slowly begin to realise the hidden potential you carry within yourself. This discovery may surprise you and might even shock you – and you may find it hard to accept at first.

The cutting-edge information presented in this book is the key to unlocking that inner potential. How you use the information is up to you. Like most people, you may simply read this book and put it aside. Or you might choose to live the rest of your life applying these powerful tools and techniques.

You have the power to make that choice. In fact, everything you are until now in your life is because of the choices you've made in your past.

When you begin to discover the natural confidence within you and your almost magical ability to take control of your life, something miraculous begins to happen. Everything and everyone turns around in your favour. No obstacle or challenge then seems to stop your way. You become what others call as ***unstoppable.***

Your journey to an unshakeable self-confidence begins with your understanding that you are the ultimate master of your own life. You are the writer, director, producer and actor of your life story. And therefore, you are free to mould it as you like.

You already have within you whatever you seek. You do not need to learn anything new. In this journey, you will only be discovering yourself. Finding your natural self-confidence within is a journey towards discovering your own hidden powerful self which is waiting to be stimulated and awakened.

If during this journey of achieving an unshakeable confidence and mastering your inner game, you ever find yourself in a dilemma or find something difficult to understand, remember that I am just an e-mail away.

Write to me at **aery@success-mantra.com** whenever you are in any confusion and I'll be glad to answer you personally!

In fact, as a gift for taking a conscious step towards your life you may write to me the most challenging problem you are facing in the path of your self-confidence and I will personally help you solve it.

So it's time to pack your bags and get started on your journey... Allow me to drive you towards success!

May you find the path to following your dreams within this book, and achieve them.

Your friend,
Aery Prabhakar

How to Read this Book

Before you begin reading this book, here are a few important things to keep in your mind:

This is an action book. You must perform all the exercises given in this book in the given order. If you do not perform the exercises, you might find yourself in a puzzle with a missing piece.

Confidence is a skill and learning it involves accepting and internalising new beliefs, habits and behaviours. It can only be done through conditioning. That involves regular repetition of targeted exercises.

Avoiding the Instant Gratification Trap. There is no magic pill. If you are looking for one and still planning to continue your search, do let me know when you find it. If somebody had it anyway, I would have dug that person out of anywhere in the world to obtain it, no matter what. However, in my intensive journey towards discovering my hidden self-confidence, I haven't found any.

The so-called magic is always a result of sheer hard work and practice and even the simplest of the performances has its own learning curve. The exercises are important – very important – as they help you create that magic in the key situations of your life.

I must repeat – exercises are really important. Do them carefully and persistently.

Get a journal for tracking your progress and your experiences in your journey towards confidence. This is very important as your mind needs to be given constant input on what exactly you want more and what you do not want any more in your life.

Before you start reading the first chapter, go through **Appendix A** at least once. It will help you tremendously in performing all the exercises in this book.

Resolve now to practise the information in this book for at least 90 days. This is the time your mind needs to assimilate and work upon all the information, develop new habits and make them permanent.

You did not learn to be under-confident overnight. However, you won't take that much time to reverse this process. The results will be apparent within a few days of practising the exercises. However, give yourself at least 3 weeks (21 days) before you start seeing any permanent results. The results are worth the effort.

And before we begin, let me assure you of the following:

Throughout this journey, I'll be with you, holding your finger and guiding you along until you are on your own.

With this, let's embark upon the journey...

For the past 33 years, I have looked in the mirror every morning and asked myself: 'If today were the last day of my life, would I want to do what I am about to do today?' And whenever the answer has been 'No' for too many days in a row, I know I need to change something.

Almost everything – all external expectations, all pride, all fear of embarrassment or failure – just falls away in the face of death, leaving only what is truly important. Remembering that you are going to die is the best way I know to avoid the trap of thinking you have something to lose.

— **STEVE JOBS,**
college dropout and
CEO of **Apple Computer,**
Stanford University Commencement, 2005

INTRODUCTION

"Self-confidence is the first requisite to great undertakings."

—Samuel Johnson

Have you ever dreamed of a life full of great health, total financial freedom, wonderful friends and fulfilling relationships?

With the unstoppable confidence you will learn to develop in this book, you can achieve it all easily!

Living a life of total self-confidence is about living fully. When you are truly confident, you radiate an inner joy, happiness and power which envelopes everything around you. You naturally attract success and abundance, and everything that you desire in your life.

The world is full of people who live their life as if they were carrying a huge burden. If you just look around, you will notice that life for most is only a source of trouble and is full of struggles, challenges and difficulties. People have learned by the virtue of the beliefs they received from society and other sources to be unsure of their own hidden abilities which can assure them a life full of joy and success.

In short, most people have lost control of their lives.

This book has been written keeping in mind the individual who wants to claim back complete control of *his or her* own life – and master his or her mental, emotional, physical and financial destiny – through the sheer and magnetic force of self-confidence.

The reality is that no story of true and lasting success was ever written without the mention of an unbeatable and unstoppable something that seemed to blast through every obstacle in its path.

It is the force of a strong self-belief – of a true, unshakeable **self-confidence.**

Self-Confidence – The Gateway to Success!

The belief that success is hard to obtain has hardened across the generations and only a few who are successful continue to be so and those who are not continue to fail. This has resulted into a poor self-confidence and self-esteem which continues to run most people's lives in the opposite direction.

Most people have accepted the fact that they cannot succeed and they prove it by being stuck where they are for their entire lives, full of uncontrollable emotions and lack of any positive energy. They are not living their lives – they are just acting like machines doing their routine work.

The problem is that they are the ones who are making all this happen all the time, designing and creating their own lives in a negative way and then blaming it on others, external conditions and circumstances.

In order to get the results you want in your life, the shift must happen inside you.

You've probably picked up this book because you have a particular problem that you would like to get resolved once and for all. It might be your social skills, your ability to communicate, in public or with the opposite sex, to feel better about yourself, to feel more worthy... and there are countless other things.

Whatever it is, it's for sure that you are here to take control of a certain area of your life.

You have taken this step by buying this book. Congratulations! By doing so, you've already qualified yourself to be worthy of success.

Extensive research conducted by the world's top psychologists over a long period has suggested that how happy and at peace we feel is proportional to the degree of control that we believe we have over our lives, i.e. over our emotions, health, relationships and finances etc.

The key is to take **CONTROL** – control of **yourself**, your emotions, your **finances**, your **relationships**, your **health** and your **mind**, even of those around you and the things that happen to you. When you know that you are in control, you don't need to worry about anything. Everything that happens does so because you have decided to let it happen.

How does it feel to be in control? Just imagine if you were in control of everything that happens in your life...how would you feel?

The reality is that you are actually controlling everything that is already happening in your life. You are ultimately responsible for all your present circumstances, the people you have in your life and the things you are achieving or not achieving. This is something that we will discuss in detail later.

I dare to say that you are the ultimate creator, designer and master of your own destiny. This is not a theory or a motivational statement. It's a Law, just like the Law of Gravity. It's invincible, immutable and timeless.

Before your mind begins to bring up the limitations that want to confront the above statements, hold on and **understand this**: Your journey to self-discovery begins by YOUR decision to follow the instructions of this book with an open mind.

When you will achieve the results that you want, you will automatically start believing in the above statements. To create a belief, you need evidence to support it. Nobody else is going to give you those evidence. You are the one who will create them for yourself.

This book will take you through the journey of self-discovery where you will uncover the hidden potential lying inside you, slowly and step by step until you meet that REAL, POWERFUL **YOU** who does not know any fear or limitation.

Do you want to meet this real, powerful and hidden YOU?

In this book, you will find the tools and resources to make that happen. However, the action part depends entirely on you. The more religiously you follow the instructions given in this book, the faster you will be able to smash your fears, master your limitations and achieve whatever you want from your life.

Usually, everything happening in our life is because we are not aware of the underlying subconscious beliefs holding us back, making us fear a potential change and even hitting us with the fear of success. There are many fears and limitations that we have learned throughout our life that act like a wall in the path of our success.

You have the power to smash this wall if you just pay attention to your subconscious habits and mindsets that you need to change in order to enjoy an unlimited self-confidence – and take massive action to replace them with positive and powerful ones.

You must know the REAL you before you achieve a rock-solid, unshakeable and unlimited self-confidence, the kind which literally puts you on the path of success and abundance, without any fear or limitations that generally come in the way.

You are in for a treat, my friend. And you'll see that for yourself.

My Personal Journey to Confidence

And now, you might be thinking, "Who is this guy who claims to teach such an important factor of life?"

Before we go any further, it's crucial that we know more about each other. After all, we are going to take this journey together. It's time we shook hands and got to know each other.

Who am I to teach you this stuff?

That's a good question, and I will do my best to answer it to your satisfaction.

Here's a quote for you from the book, *Illusions – The Adventures of a Reluctant Messiah*: **"We teach best what we need to learn the most."**

My life has been a quest to discover the confidence within me which would allow me to express myself fully to the external world, make friends, laugh, find a soul mate, achieve success and feel worthy of being here on this earth.

I was the kind of guy you could call a nerd or geek (or any other nasty word you like to use, it's OK, it doesn't hurt me anymore). Locked up in my room, I only used to wonder how it is like to be a part of a great group of friends, to communicate confidently with the women I desire, to believe that I too, can be successful in life and to feel worthy of all great things in life.

Whenever there was an opportunity to make a presence or come out in front of the world, I always stood frozen, as if tied tightly by steel ropes.

On encountering an attractive woman I would fill with shame and embarrassment for my 'dirty' desires. Worst of all, there was a deep hidden fear of being caught for my desires that seemed to emerge out of nowhere.

I had no friends. People whom I knew were living as loathsome a life as mine. Life cannot get worse than this. Loneliness can kill, really.

Somewhere inside, I had always wanted to make my presence felt. I always wanted to communicate with total confidence, have friends, have fun as others did and enjoy total control over the way I felt. In short, I wanted to feel normal and in **control** of my life.

At that particular time though, it was all just a fantasy for me. A fantasy I dwelled upon every day, every moment and wondered if I would ever achieve these abilities.

I was convinced that everything in my life was happening by the will of some unseen power who didn't like me for some reason and that I was just an innocent soul being tortured in this world.

When I look back today, having learned that we are ultimately the cause of everything going on in our lives, I can't help but laugh at the way I allowed myself to feel.

Your situation may not be as bad as mine, but I hope you get the picture.

How This Book is Different

This book is unlike other programmes available on boosting your self-confidence. If it wasn't, I wouldn't write it – simple.

"There is an inner game of EVERYTHING," said W. Timothy Gallwey, the author of the famous *Inner Game* series. His works include *The Inner Game of Golf*, *The Inner Game of Work* and *The Inner Game of Music*.

The Inner game is a synergistic combination of internal mindsets and belief systems which dramatically affect your actions, thoughts, and speech.

What I have come to understand is that there's also an **Inner Game of Confidence** which is generally ignored in the midst of the chaos of fast techniques and quick fixes to obtain social mastery.

The problem of wanting instant gratification – to have something right when you want it is the main culprit of this problem. As I said before, there's no magic pill.

You can 'fake it until you make it' and make your life even harder without ever knowing the real reason for the things going wrong. You can learn a few fast techniques which help you create instant rapport with and make others like you and still never get what you really want.

This book doesn't give you 'Smile to please' and 'Listen intently to make others like you' techniques. Those things are mentioned and discussed in relevant sections but with the assumption that they are too obvious in nature.

Clearly, the problem is something else. For example, what can a smile do when it comes from a frame of mind which shouts desperation and weakness?

Imagine a guy feebly trying to force a smile at a girl he likes, clearly to seek her approval. Women are attracted to men who have a strong sense of self and this guy just blew it. You know what will happen next. You have probably seen this irritating smile on the face of the cunning door-to-door salesman who's trying to sell you a cheap, useless product and probably knows it's worthless. It's like buying a great looking car with no engine inside it. There is simply no power that could drive it.

You cannot make anyone like you or produce any **positive and permanent results** without setting your **inner game** right. In order to produce a real, lasting and unshakeable self-confidence within you, the shift must occur deep inside you where your subconscious mindsets, beliefs and behaviours rest.

When you are truly confident and in control of your inner reality, you automatically begin to obtain the necessary skills needed for mastery in every area of your life. A confident human being is compelled to learn these things as a necessary part of life. Every new learning in the life of a confident human being is a natural and effortless process of self-discovery.

Most of my discoveries has come from an intensive personal delving into the realm of human psychology and consistently applying all that I learned. During all this time, I have been carefully observing myself and those I have been fortunate enough to help create better lives for themselves.

I have really enjoyed and devoured every moment since I started this incredible journey of discovering self-confidence within me. Out of this journey has originated a concrete, straightforward and easy to follow system for developing an unshakeable confidence within anyone who follows it. This book contains that system. Follow it and take control of your life.

1

AWAKENING OF THE CONFIDENCE WITHIN

"If you think you can, you can. And if you think you can't, you're right."

—Henry Ford

No wonder this confident man put the wheels of modern automobiles in motion and also acted as a powerful catalyst to the 20th century economy and society.

In today's world, it is so important to spruce up one's confidence levels that one simply cannot afford to ignore it. In order to be, do or have anything worthwhile in life, one must possess sufficient amount of self-confidence.

"Desire is the starting point of all achievements", said Napoleon Hill in his classic *Think and Grow Rich*. However, he also mentions in a later chapter that the biggest obstacle in achieving your deepest desires is a lack of confidence. Your dreams are as good as nothing if they aren't followed up with massive action.

All positive and consistent action – the kind that produces real results stems from a strong foundation of self-confidence. Confidence is the starting point of all action and hence, all the worthy results you produce in your lifetime.

Why Self-Confidence?

It is my belief that self-confidence is the factor which determines what level, quality and kind of life you're going to spend.

With an unshakeable self-confidence, you will become a conscious designer of your own life. No matter how many obstacles come your way or difficulties try to sway you, your unshakeable faith in yourself will keep you calm, certain and powerful in the face of everything.

With greater self-confidence, you will be able to set higher goals for yourself and actually achieve them!

With greater self-confidence, you will be able to manage your unconscious conflicts and smooth up your life.

With an unshakeable self-confidence, you will be able to claim back total control of your life. The feeling of total control also brings the feeling of true happiness and a sense of calm inside you – the signs of a fully confident human being.

With an unstoppable self-confidence, you will always be full of everlasting energy. You would be able to take massive actions towards your goals and have fun while you accomplish each and every goal you set for yourself.

You may be...

- a seeker aspiring to learn a new skill and need a boost of confidence...
- someone who is unsure of your life and desires to get focused, boost your self-esteem and self-image.
- a student aspiring to achieve greater results in your academic life.
- a lover wanting to gather enough confidence to just 'say it'. (It's easier than you think!).
- a man or a woman who desires to be able to easily attract the opposite sex.
- a salesman aspiring to be really able to 'sell' something or may be you are already good and want to achieve excellence.
- a worker who wants to qualify for a promotion and fears his boss or simply wants to feel he deserves when he asks for it.

Or...

- You may be going through a period of setbacks or failures in your life and want to claim the control of your life back.

- You may want to become more organised, more focused and more confident in your life.

No matter who you are and what you want in your life and regardless of what your past has been, it doesn't matter. All you need is right direction. And I am here to give you just that.

What is NOT Confidence!

Confidence is not a **quality.** It's not something you have or possess. It's not a **talent.**

Confidence is not **arrogance**. Arrogance is simply an egoistic attitude towards the world, usually accompanied by other negative thoughts about oneself and others like a deep-rooted insecurity(s) about something or a superiority complex.

Confidence is different from **self-esteem**. Self-esteem means 'appreciating your own worth and importance' – and it helps you to cope better with the challenges of life. It's a belief in your own self-worth and importance.

Confidence – The Real Definition

To begin the path of attaining rock solid, unshakeable self-confidence, it's important to understand its underlying meaning.

What exactly is **self-confidence?**

The Webster Dictionary defines the term 'confidence' as: 1) a firm belief; trust; reliance; 2) the fact of being or feeling certain; assurance; 3) belief in one's own abilities; self-confidence

Everyone has his or her own definition of confidence. For an athlete, it might be the ability to stay calm and composed on the big day. For a young man, it might be the ability to approach someone from the opposite sex. For a speaker, it might be the ability to speak fearlessly and powerfully in front of a large group and get a standing ovation.

However, all the above things are the 'results' of an unshakeable self-confidence, just like side effects albeit positive ones.

Confidence is a firm belief in your ability to make anything you want happen. When you know deep down inside that you can make something happen, in spite of all the obstacles you may have to master in order to accomplish it, you are confident.

Confidence is a **state of mind**. It's a **FEELING**. Just think how you feel about doing something you are really good at. For many people it could be just driving. It might be something else for you, like a sport.

Do you feel a sense of certainty about it? Come on, you just know you can do it. It's so obvious to you. That's confidence.

If you have a glass of water in front of you and you feel thirsty, how confident you are that you'll simply extend your hand, pick up the glass and drink the water? You can easily do it. After all, you have done it so many times in your life.

Are you beginning to understand what I am trying to convey here? Until now, you are probably unsure of your own level of self-confidence. So here's where your journey begins. In order to get somewhere, you must know where you are at this moment.

We'll start by finding out your present levels of self-confidence. First of all, go to the last section of this book and take the confidence quiz on page 168 When you are done and have your results, come back and continue reading.

What? Are you still here?

Well sorry for doubting you – but **IT'S IMPORTANT!** If you haven't taken the quiz yet, go do it first.

Welcome back!

So how were the results?

Now you know exactly where you stand at this particular moment of time. You know where you are in the journey right now.

The Causes of Low-Confidence

Many of us mistakenly associate lack of skill with lack of confidence.

If you fear public speaking, it's because you need to learn and practise what it takes to be a good public speaker. You need to know how to manage your specific fears and instead turn them into something which can empower you. Public speaking is a skill. **If you aren't good at it, this has nothing to do with your confidence.**

I have personally experienced and seen countless number of people attaching their whole life to a particular skill they lack, and instead of learning and mastering it they go on to sabotage their own success and in many cases, their entire lives.

An example are those men who don't understand that meeting and attracting the woman they want can be a skill (which it is) and has nothing to do with their being worthless or inadequate. The same goes for women who are a little too confused about how they can attract the kind of man they want in their lives.

Again, you don't need a fix. You need a new strategy.

The Difference That Makes the Difference

It's time for some action. Take a pen/pencil and your journal.

The chart given below clearly demonstrates the key differences between a confident and a non-confident human being. Go through the chart carefully and notice your own problems and strengths. Mark them as you read.

Non-Confident Human Being

- A continuous, uncontrollable need for attention and approval from everyone.
- Lives and acts out of fear of rejection/failure.
- Vulnerable to all kinds of fears.
- A need to be perfect and right all the time. A deep, inner desire of being 'better than others', no matter what it takes.
- Inability to take decisions.
- Inability to express oneself assertively.
- Can get emotionally immobilised or stuck in key situations of life.
- Negative, submissive body language. Inability to see others in eyes. Wrong posture.

- Lack of energy in voice tone. Weak, timid and sometimes squeaking voice.
- Uncontrollable nervousness, sweating.
- Fearful of conflicts; arguments. Fear confrontations.
- A liar. Usually tells lies for defence.
- Inability to take and carry on responsibilities.
- Dependence on drugs, sex, porn, smoking or other such things for mental fulfilment.
- Arrogant, angry and controlling.
- Has no or poorly defined goals.
- Disconnected from one's ultimate purpose of life or possibly, has no idea that it exists.
- Feeling of unworthiness and loneliness; a need to be accepted by others.
- Shame, guilt and regret for one's sexual desires.
- Tense, anxious and uptight around others.
- Inability to carry on a conversation even when desired.
- Negative beliefs about oneself and others; reinforces himself negatively; negative self-talk.
- Immaturity, childishness (or over seriousness).
- Lack of consistency, persistence and will power; can't handle setbacks.
- Revengeful; suspicious nature.

The Confident Human Being

- Has compelling goals that powerfully inspire & excite.
- Is growing consciously in all areas of life – emotional, financial and physical.
- Is proactive. Makes things happen by going for them.
- Has an internal locus of control – only bothers about things which are directly under control.
- Has mastered the worry habit – for good!

- Knows how to manage his feelings and emotions and use them to achieve his goals.
- Is totally comfortable with self, others and in any social situation.
- Laughs comfortably; has relaxed and powerful body language and makes strong eye contact.
- Lives in alignment with his deepest values and beliefs and never strays from them.
- Is decisive and an independent thinker.
- Is comfortable around opposite sex and with one's sexuality.
- Is sexually confident and has a healthy sexual attitude.
- Powerful and impressive body language and voice tone.
- A powerful eye contact.
- Ability to see the funny side of life; good sense of humour.
- Can say 'No' without feeling bad – a sign of 'assertiveness'.
- Is comfortable with his own views, beliefs & opinions.
- Has a deep self-respect and expects others to respect him/her too.
- Respects others opinions and doesn't feel a need to prove himself to others.
- Does not tolerate disrespect to himself and his time.
- Takes life as an adventure. Consider challenges as opportunities to learn, grow & have fun.
- Truly believes in self; knows that he/she deserve just the best in life.
- Lives the present to its fullest; understands that the past is dead and future hasn't arrived yet.
- Has a healthy self-image; takes care of his clothing, looks and grooming.
- Knows how to stay motivated.
- Is a good manager, in relationships, business/work and personal life.
- Is a motivator; helps others achieve their dreams.
- Is a leader; knows how to takes decisions for others.

These lists project a complete difference in the attitudes, behaviours and beliefs of a non-confident & confident human being.

The difference is staggering. It's like two human beings on totally different dimensions.

Most people on this earth are exhibiting the features in the first list. Is it any wonder why only a few people succeed in life?

If you can learn to unlearn the habits which undermine confidence and replace them with new habits you will automatically become self-confident. It is here where the promise of 'magic pills' fails.

This is not an overnight job, although the tools and techniques you will learn in this book will shorten the curve from years to just a few days.

Self-confidence, just like success, is like a journey. It continues to increase forever as you incorporate and strengthen new attitudes, beliefs, habits and behaviours inside you.

Get Ready to Awaken... it's Time for Change!

Imagine a bee smashing its head against the mirror hoping to break through it. It does it again and again with the hope that the path will open up, when in reality just a little above the mirror a window might be open, or a door may be open somewhere around. But for the bee, it doesn't even exist.

As long as the bee will continue to bang its head against the glass, she will never get through it. She has to change her approach and find another way.

Do you know the definition of madness? It's doing one thing again and again and expecting different results every time. Most people in this world will agree with this; and yet this is exactly what most of the world is doing all the time.

The only thing permanent on this planet is 'change'. Your journey towards an unstoppable self-confidence begins with your decision to change yourself.

There is a famous saying: 'We all want to go to heaven, but nobody wants to die.' Unless you are a special guest of the lords who are running the world, it makes sense to die first.

Give Up Your Resistance to Change

Everybody in the world wants to become successful, to achieve abundance and prosperity in life but we all resist change. The reality is that the only permanent thing in this world is change. Everything around us and inside us is changing. We are all either growing or falling every moment.

Resistance to change comes from a natural internal mechanism which tries to protect you from the external world. You wouldn't want to learn driving every three days because you forgot how to drive. Would you?

In order to become successful and live life fully, you must break out of your old comfort zone. This comfort zone is what keeps you trapped inside your skin, away from the adventures and thrills of life, and instead create a problematic, frustrating life.

Finding that real, natural confidence within you can be accomplished easily if you decide now to change.

When something isn't working in your life anymore and needs to be changed consciously, your mind will still resist at first.

This is exactly why:

1. The first time you do anything, it seems very difficult. It doesn't feel like YOU. In short, 'it's not who you are'.
2. The second time you do something, it is easier than the first time.
3. The more you do something repeatedly and let your mind and body come together in a congruent pattern which eventually becomes habitual and a neural pathway is formed in your brain, the easier it becomes.
4. Eventually, the new habit becomes a permanent part of YOU.

Ask yourself these questions now:

'Am I willing to change now?'

'Am I willing to do whatever it takes to create this change?'

Either you are going to feel totally sure of yourself or you will experience an inner resistance. If you feel it, it's time to talk to your inner self. Your inner self is at some level comfortable with the present conditions and circumstances and derives some pleasure out of it.

Don't just assume you are ready to change based on your excitement. Pay attention to the signals your unconscious is trying to give you through body feelings. Do you feel a sense of being 'stuck' or 'not really that sure' somewhere inside? That's a block your unconscious is trying to put in the path of your change.

If it is so, you need to have a face to face talk with your unconscious.

EXERCISE

Connect Massive Pain to Your Present Way of Thinking

This is an exercise. Please use a pen / pencil and your journal.

In order to break through this inner resistance, you need to create enough pain for the present conditions. Let me ask you a question…

'Where will you be in the next 6 months, 1 year and finally 2 years if you do not step forward to change now?'

Think about all the things you will be losing and missing in your life. Great friends, relationships, financial success, love, adventures, thrill… anything that drives you.

Close your eyes and picture yourself experiencing the lack.

Connect massive pain to not changing right now. Go a step ahead and see yourself living a life full of frustration. Look back to this time and wonder what you could have accomplished if you had decided to change.

Picture yourself five years from now…and see where you'll be if you do **NOT** change and continue to be who you are today… see the things you'll be missing, great relationships you could've had, financial success…

What will you miss emotionally, physically and mentally if you do not make that decision now?

Remember, pain is the key to initiate the process of change. Human minds by some default setting avoid pain and run towards pleasure.

Open your eyes. Once you have done that, come back and thank yourself that you are still here. Thank yourself for being able to make the right changes now. You can still choose to change.

Connect Extreme Pleasure To Changing Now!

What if you decide to change now? Now, as you continue to read these words...close your eyes again and see yourself full of an unshakeable and unstoppable self-confidence. See yourself accomplishing all great things in your life you want with your new found self-confidence.

Picture yourself five years from now... See yourself living in total abundance, having great relationships and succeeding just the way you want to. See yourself having wonderful friends, financial freedom and everything else that you could ever want in your life.

You can have it all if you choose to change **now.**

Are you willing to change now? If yes, go ahead and give yourself a cheer. Give yourself a little pat or may be a treat to a dinner or a movie. Whatever it is, do anything that makes you feel wonderful. Let your mind know the importance of this decision.

Understand this: Change is only painful in the short term. We as human beings are all resistant to change. That's why we see only a handful of people living fully. Since you have decided to be one of them, you must understand that it's YOU who is going to bring the change in yourself. Nobody else can do it for you.

When You Really Want Something – You Get It!

So far in your life, you've always got what you have really wanted. If there was ever something you wanted so badly you couldn't live without it in your past, you have it now. Most probably you couldn't stop thinking about it and continuously imagining the pleasures of having it in your mind.

Whatever it is you haven't got yet in spite of all your efforts, it's something you aren't really committed about making happen, if not consciously, then at some unconscious level.

It was because you were committed and even if you had to sell your piggy bank to get it – you did it. Commitment may sound like a boring word with a touch of rigidity to it but in reality, it is what ultimately matters.

How committed are you towards building your self-confidence?

There has to be the power of commitment at work behind you while you are on your journey towards an unshakeable self-confidence.

So write your name, the level of confidence you want to achieve and the reason(s) you want to achieve it, below.

> **"I** ____________________(your name), **have decided I want to create a rock solid, unshakeable and unstoppable self-confidence, which will lead me to the life of my ultimate dreams, because** ____________________**, and I'm committed to following the instructions given in this book until I have reached my desired level of confidence"**

In Conclusion

I have a little anecdote I saved for the end of this chapter. Featured in the *Seven Habits of Highly Effective People* (by **Stephen R. Covey**), it conveys something very important.

'Two battleships assigned to the training squadron had been at sea on manoeuvres in heavy weather for several days. I was serving on the lead battleship and was on watch on the bridge as night fell. The visibility was poor with patchy fog, so the captain remained on the bridge keeping an eye on all activities.

Shortly after dark, the lookout on the wing of the bridge reported, "Light, bearing on the starboard bow."

"Is it steady or moving astern?" the captain yelled out.

Lookout replied, "Steady, captain," which meant we were on a dangerous collision course with that ship.

The captain then called to the signalman, "Signal that ship: We are on a collision course, advise you change course 20 degrees."

Back came a signal, "Advisable for you to change course 20 degrees."

The captain said, "Send, I'm a captain, change course 20 degrees."

"I'm a seaman second class," came the reply. "You had better change course 20 degrees."

By that time, the captain was furious. He spat out, "Send, I'm a battleship. Change course 20 degrees."

Back came the flashing light, "I'm a lighthouse."

We changed course.'

Remember, the world won't change for you. So don't try to change it. **Change yourself...**that's what you can do most efficiently and anytime you want.

Change yourself and the whole world will change with you. That's an astounding fact which you're about to experience.

Keep this in your mind as you read the rest of this book.

2

WHAT'S HOLDING YOU BACK

*"Somebody should tell us right at the start of our lives that we are dying... Then, we might live life to the limit! Every minute of every day! **Do it, I say!** Whatever it is you want to do, **Do it now!** There are only so many tomorrows..."*

—Actor **Michael Landon**, afflicted with terminal pancreatic cancer, in a 1991 *Life* interview.

The Journey through Childhood

There is a time in everyone's life when we are free of all limitations.

I am talking about your childhood – when everything was possible. In that time, there was an unrestricted curiosity and unending desire to explore the world fully, completely and limitlessly.

When I look back to my childhood, I remember the time when I used to climb on my rooftop, extend my hand towards the sky and jump in desperation so that I can touch that stunning blue sky that seemed to be so out of reach. "There has to be a way", I would groan.

"How far it could be?" I used to think relentlessly.

Little did I know how the space scientists all around the world had not only touched that beautiful blue sky but had surpassed it already, travelling to distant planets and exploring them to their farthest limits.

Is there really such a thing as impossible?

Not a long time ago, I was attending a seminar organised by a popular network marketing company. The speaker (whose name I don't remember) had us all hypnotised with his amazing inspirational stories and excellent speaking skills. He was a man of refined excellence, having already paved his path through the challenges of network marketing success.

At the end of his speech, he said, "Is there anyone who believes that human beings can fly, without any external help?"

There was a silence.

"May be you can do it. We all can do it, if we just begin to believe in it enough. The day isn't far away. Trust me", he said, with a passion and belief in his eyes that has to be seen in person to realise its power.

His words penetrated in my heart like an arrow shot straight in the bull's eye. It was at that moment the memories of childhood, of me trying to touch that sky appeared from nowhere.

Think of your own childhood. Go back to that time when regardless of circumstances around you, you were connected to your inner joy and confidence. Everything was possible at that wonderful time of life.

As you grew, however, you started becoming aware of the world around you. Something seemed to be seriously wrong with people. You noticed them consciously and unconsciously, struggling with their lives and living as if depression, problems and challenges were a normal and natural part of life.

By being with them and mostly guided by the same people to help create your beliefs and understandings about your life, you started to develop personal beliefs which were opposite to what you used to believe back in your childhood.

We tend to identify with everyone who has had a dominant effect on our lives during our childhood which is a period of mental and physical growth. They can be your parents, teachers or any other authority figures who taught you things that you thought were right. Even if you found something wrong, you had no other choice but to follow the instructions. If they are doing it all the time, it must be right!

Ouch!

The dreams seen in the eye of childhood were buried down under the layers of false beliefs and limitations.

A large part of human race today is running around living a life full of false beliefs and limitations. There is no wonder that inferiority and inadequacy is a normal part of our lives. These false beliefs cause a lack of faith in oneself and the surrounding world.

The end result is a poor self-confidence and self-esteem.

In chapter 6, you'll receive instructions to identify and resolve your limiting beliefs. For now, just realise that your beliefs are playing a very important part in your present levels of self-confidence.

Do You Fear Success?

It's mind-blowing to know but for many people, being successful in life also equals something negative in life.

If you are fearful of success in your life and believe that success has a negative side to it, you will have a very hard time getting successful.

If you have negative unconscious associations with success or achieving self-confidence, your mind will keep on sabotaging your own success.

You wouldn't want to let that happen, would you?

The Secret Identity of a Failure

People who fear success are identified with the wrong mindsets and beliefs that prevent them from having what they want in their lives. If you are carrying this fear inside you, you can identify it by answering the following questions.

1. **Do you believe that success often comes the hard way and is reserved for those who are rich, have a successful background or are plain lucky?**
2. **Do you believe that for achieving any kind of success in your life, you must work exceptionally hard?**
3. **Do you believe that you are a far better being where you are right now since you have no big responsibilities and therefore problems that come with success?**

If you answered 'yes' to any of the above questions, you are probably running your life with brakes on. Remember, an enemy discovered is an enemy half whipped. When you know what is stopping you from becoming super confident, you can be better prepared to eliminate it from your life forever.

Your awareness is enough to dissolve these obstacles away from your path. Most probably, you have no idea what powers you are holding inside you.

Within each of us is the ability to turn around any situation of your life into our favour, attain mastery in whatever we want, achieve anything we aspire and create anything we desire.

If that sounds unbelievable, guess what is making you feel like that– your own limiting beliefs, internal fears and habitual thoughts.

A Meeting With Your Subconscious Mind

Your subconscious is your hidden reservoir of everything that has ever happened in your life. It contains all your inner beliefs and habits that govern your life.

In the context of self-confidence, let us now discuss one of the most important laws that govern our entire life. It is the law of habit.

The law of habit states that anything that is repeated time and again by us is eventually taken up by the subconscious mind and can be seen in the outward/bodily actions of that person, finally leading to a physical establishment of the thought in reality.

The law of habit works directly in conjunction with the human mind, creating a neural pathway in the brain each time a particular action is taken.

A **NEURAL PATHWAY** can be referred to a simple path in your brain that has been built by forcing your mind in a particular direction and eventually you find all your thoughts going in that very direction automatically and effortlessly, like driving or falling in love.

With every repetition, a new thread is formed adding strength to the neural pathway. This pathway, these threads are not just hypothetical. They are REAL! They exist in REAL physical form inside our brains.

Confidence is nothing but a set of positive, useful neural pathways which determine your habits.

Confidence can be developed by replacing your old set of habits with new ones. You do it by destroying the old neural pathways and

REPLACING them with new ones. This is true for any other habit you would like to replace or build.

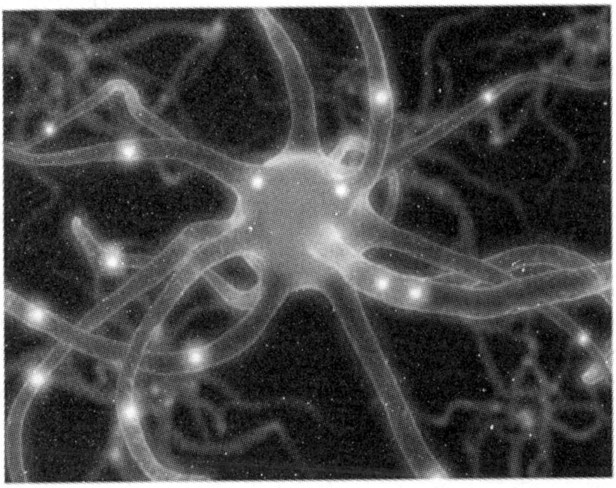

Neural Pathways (Source: mindfulnesstennis.com)

The question here is how we form our desired pathways. Those that lead us to positive and powerful states and make us exhibit a spectacular confidence and ease in all the situations.

The key is to understand how the neural pathways that are already in our mind were made in the first place. Let's take a look at a great example that will help us expand our knowledge on this spectacular subject.

The 'Falling In Love' Analogy

Have you ever been in love with someone? If you have, you probably can identify with the following stages:

1. You felt fascinated towards the desired person and kept thinking about him/her since it felt really pleasurable. This fascination slowly grew so strong in a short time that you found yourself thinking of that person most of the time on autopilot.
2. The desire was multiplied with time. Your mind created a powerful image of the beloved. When this happens.....

The DESIRE and the fascination of that object/ person is so strong that it leads to a strange state of mind where a neural pathway, rather an expressway is created and you are emotionally hypnotised.

The neural states are so strong that whatever you do, your thoughts run towards the direction of your own created pathway and hence to the image of the person. The attachment to the 'image' of the person becomes uncontrollable and is continuously reinforced.

If you have noticed already, I said 'Image' – not the real person. The human mind doesn't have the ability to distinguish between a real-world experience and a intensive, detailed visualisation.

A common man who does not understand the principles of human mind and especially attraction and lacks sufficient self-confidence may also keep on fearing that he might lose his beloved. Since the focus is on negative, the ultimate result is also negative in nature. What you focus upon expands.

This fear becomes a part of his unconscious mind, making the emotions even more intense and ultimately leading to even more fascination towards the object/ person he desires.

Understand this: A habit can only be replaced. It cannot be destroyed. Human brain simply needs another neural pathway in place of the old one. There is no place for a vacuum.

Also, the more you want a thing, the more powerful will be the emotions involved and the more speedily the results will come.

The old neural pathways your mind is so accustomed to travel will wear away and disappear and you will be left with new neural pathways which you have consciously chosen.

EXERCISE

The following exercise is designed to flawlessly communicate with your subconscious and easily make desired changes in it, almost effortlessly.

Your subconscious is an integral (and powerful!) part of YOU and is always eager to listen to you. In some or the other way, it is always communicating with you. It may be through body feelings, or intuitions or a sudden thought. When you pay attention to it and call it for assistance, it immediately listens.

You may have trouble a first few times understanding its signals due to the noisy chatter which always goes on in your mind but eventually, communicating with your subconscious will become a normal process for you.

Do not be afraid of the strange and new sensations or experiences you may feel during this exercise. It's your subconscious trying to communicate with you. Welcome the new feelings.

This exercise will take around 30 minutes of your time, during which you must ensure that your are not interrupted in any way.

Write down a complete description of your future self when you will have achieved the levels of self-confidence you want. Keep these points in mind when you write...

- Don't rush. You are designing your own life here; do it carefully. Make a clear picture of what you want.
- Be specific. You can use the questions given below to help yourself in writing. The key is to just keep writing without thinking or editing. Remember, details are important. Write for at least 15 minutes non-stop, (or until your mind totally gives up) as if your life depends upon it. (It actually does).
- Don't think of any limitations. Be free to write whatever you really want. Think like a child.

Questions to aid you in creating the description:

If you had the confidence you want...

1. What would you dare to make happen?
2. How will you carry yourself?
3. What will you be wearing?
4. How would you be breathing?
5. What things would you be able to accomplish?
6. What kind of energy you will exude? Positive, powerful, vibrating, fun, magnetic?
7. What will be your beliefs about yourself, your life, the world and the people around you?
8. How will you treat your inferiors?

9. How will you deal with your superiors?
10. How will you deal with your employees? (If you intend to be an employer)
11. How will you respond to something that makes you angry?
12. How will you handle negative, challenging situations?
13. How will you handle setbacks in your life?
14. How will you handle your relationships?
15. What things will you do when you are just with yourself?
16. What will be your general attitude towards life?
17. What kind of sense of humour would you have?
18. How will you deal with the opposite sex? How will the opposite sex treat you?
19. How other people will treat you?
20. How will you treat other people?
21. What will be your financial position?

Add any other things that you like. Be as detailed as you can.

Now when you are done, read your description carefully. Form a mental picture of your desired confident self out of it. Imagine that you are sitting in a theatre and watching a movie of you acting like you would when you have the kind of confidence you desire.

On a scale of 1-10, rate how well this picture motivates you. If it's less than 10, fine-tune your picture until it becomes a 10. Fill details, pictures, sounds, smells and feelings. If you have a trouble visualising in detail or visualising at all, see **Appendix A** for help.

Once you have it, rewrite your description so that it depicts your fine tuned picture you just imagined above.

Close your eyes. This is the most important part so make sure you have no distractions. If required, put a 'Do not Disturb' sign on your door.

Focus your attention inward. Ask your subconscious to communicate with you. I usually say, "My subconscious mind, I request you to come forward and talk to me in conscious." Use any statement that feels as powerful to you. Just watch your feelings, they reveal everything.

Repeat this three times and notice the feelings. If the feelings seem positive, then you are on the right track. If not, say it again three times.

You will know when your subconscious is ready to talk to you. You may have shivering sensations or a deep inner feeling of affirmation. It's a nod of affirmation from your subconscious. It's now ready to talk to you in conscious.

Look at your description and bring back the picture you created above. Say these words three times to your subconscious:

"This is what I want to be, do and have when I'll have achieved my ideal confident self."

Now ask your subconscious to provide you with the time that'll be required to make this picture a reality. You will have a hunch, a feeling that gives you that time frame. If you don't get it at the first attempt, persist. Ask it to give you this time frame.

Whatever you receive, write it down. Confirm this time frame by asking "Is this what you just communicated? Have I correctly interpreted it?"

If you feel a 'Yes' coming from inside then we're done with the exercise. If there's a doubt or a straight 'NO', ask it again to provide you with a new time frame. Repeat the process.

After you are done, thank your subconscious and slowly open your eyes.

Everyday, just before going to sleep and right after you wake up in the morning, read this description and create a mental movie of yourself with all the qualities above and see yourself doing things just the way you would want to do. It should not take more than 5 minutes. Do this for 90 days straight.

Remember, you must make this an **associated experience.** See **Appendix A** to understand what an associated experience is.

While you do this, focus on that one thing that you most desire to accomplish with your new found Self-Confidence. See yourself doing that thing perfectly. End your session with successfully executing this one special thing you want for yourself.

3

KILL THE VICTIM INSIDE

"Nothing has more power over you than you allow it to be."

We all have an unknown something living inside us which seems to be running our lives. It makes us believe that whenever something wrong or bad happens, it's probably due to some unknown force which doesn't like us and is controlling each and every event happening in our life.

It's sad to hear people sometimes, complaining about their unending troubles and problems. However, if you listen carefully, there is an amazingly funny pattern you will begin to find. Everything they complain about is a result of the same old belief which says: 'You are doomed because you are unlucky'.

If you are a complainer yourself, pay attention to your own inner belief driving your dissatisfaction from your life.

Obviously some problems are real. Somebody has tried but failed to secure a job, the other is unhappy in his or her present job, someone doesn't have the love of their spouses and others do not even have someone who loves them. Everyone is lacking something and it is often defined as the reason to be unhappy.

In fact, many people live their lives as if it was a great liability.

It's easy to find people walking around with their heads down and accepting whatever life seems to be giving them, usually which is just a leftover of what the powerful and **successful** who already have what they want. After all, they believe, there's a limit to everything.

And on top of that, almost everyone seems to be in a great hurry; trying to secure their place in the world before anyone else can.

'It's a cutthroat competition and winning takes effort and cunningness' – is what they seem to believe.

You must have wondered sometime, why is the majority of world living like that? What is it that makes them feel like a victim to the outer conditions, circumstances and to the people of authority who seem to control them?

I used to wonder about this as well, until I found to my amazement the staggering truth behind all the above mess.

You Are the Ultimate Controller

Nothing in your life should happen without your permission, and let me tell you that, it actually never happens without your permission.

You might not be consciously aware of something you are permitting unconsciously in your life. If you aren't able to get your finances right, for example, in spite of your best efforts – there's a clear conflict between your conscious desires and unconscious beliefs.

You are the master of your own life: This is not a motivational statement to fire you up. It is a law of the universe. This is how it has chosen to operate itself, to follow your own deepest desires and longings and bring them to you in their physical forms.

The problem is that most of the times, while we think we want something else, something inside us tends to disagree again and again, and we don't get it. May be it's not what you **really** want.

This indicates a clear disagreement between your conscious and unconscious mind.

Here's a little fun experiment for you. Just look around the room you are sitting in, and notice only the things in red colour.

Done?

Now close your eyes and tell me, honestly, without looking around, "What was it that was green?" Go ahead, close your eyes and try to remember.

Got a problem there? Eh.

You specifically ordered your mind to see just the RED colour and it did so by excluding all other irrelevant information. Now just think of this. If you were to create a robot which could just identify a particular colour whenever it was commanded to do so, what cost, energy and time would it take to do so?

It's amazing that you can do that. It's amazing that ANYONE can do that. Yet most people around this world aren't aware of their inner powers and abilities and are living like a diffused bomb that could explode only if it knew its capability.

You carry the most powerful computing system that could ever exist in physical form – in your own head, containing at least 1 billion cells, enough to put to shame even the most powerful computers on this earth; and yet you feel low, out of form and weary.

Does it have to be explained that your ability to feel low, out of form and weary is also a choice that you have made using your own brain and that it's you who instructed your brain cells to work in that direction?

Even your way of living like this is a matter of choice and a representation of how powerful you are.

Living with the idea that **'I don't believe in myself'** is also a belief. The system works perfectly every time.

When you walk around on this earth with a set of habits, beliefs and problems which literally scream 'I am a loser', you are being a victim. And a victim lacks the most important factor of living one's own life to the fullest, **control.**

The key word is **control.** By choosing to take control of what you do with your life and how others behave with you, you master the first pre-requisite to an unshakeable self-confidence.

A person who comes home every day and fights with his wife, scolds his children and literally makes a hell out of every 'could-be-pleasant' evening – is a victim trying to take control, at least where he can.

We all know at least one person like that. I know more than one, actually plenty of them. It could be your next door neighbour. It could be someone in your own family. It could be you as well.

We are all striving to take control of our lives; of its different aspects – be it our finances, relationships or anything else. And when someone fails to do so, his mind tries to create an illusion of control, just like in the above cases.

Tell me, honestly, how many times you find yourself living as a victim would.

Do you find an insatiable need to prove yourself to others?

Do you fear someone would feel bad, angry or disgusted at you because you said 'NO' to them?

Are you always wondering and afraid of what others are thinking about you?

Are you unable to stand for yourself whenever you are victimised by the outer world, in form of ruthless advertising, sales people, over-charging restaurants, careless drivers and friends who would get upset if you didn't do what they expect from you?

Do you let others take advantage of you and don't know how to counteract it?

Do you find it hard to communicate what you want effectively?

Do you spend time wondering about what you 'could' have said or done in a situation rather than improve upon what you actually did?

There are many other things that can help you reveal your personal identity as a victim, which most of the times is hiding somewhere deep inside you.

It's not purely visible. It needn't be. It's more effective being hidden there, controlling your life the way you don't like it. But as you put your hand to clutch its throat and pull it out, it will disappear as if it never existed.

Have You Identified Yourself as a Victim?

How do you see yourself? When you look in the mirror, what do you see? Who do you see? A winner? A successful person? Someone in control of his/her life?

Or...

A loser... a victim who is controlled by the outer circumstances and conditions of life? having no inner locus of control and trying VERY hard to come up to the expectations of others?

There's a famous saying that goes like this, "An enemy discovered is an enemy half whipped."

I was amazed to discover self-defeating patterns which declared me a victim and controlled my entire life when I started my own journey towards self-confidence.

At first, revealing those patterns put me on the defensive. They made me angry, to the point where I refused to accept their existence. Though somewhere inside I knew these patterns were running my life, it was just a little too hard to accept them.

But in the next few days, something magical happened...

My awareness began to pay off dramatically. I began to notice every pattern emerging in all my behaviours in key situations of my life. And as I noticed, I also began to correct myself. After doing that a few times, the patterns began to disappear automatically and starting getting replaced with powerful, confident patterns.

This is true with all your false beliefs you have been hypnotised into and your old mindsets and behaviours. They make your life a tough hill to climb and make you crawl. The moment you know the truth about them, they will cease to exist.

So let's go find out how to de-victimise yourself from your old patterns, once and forever!

I want you to begin thinking of these patterns as you go through them as they apply in your own life. As you read them, go back in your past and think where you displayed them and how can you replace them in the future comings.

The Beliefs of a Victim

1. There is no use in trying – I know I'm going to lose.

This sentence rings in the mind of a victim whenever he/she is trying to accomplish something worthwhile, and which is out of normal comfort zone.

If you can hear your mind literally shout "I'm going to lose anyway" whenever you are about to give that important presentation, approach the one you admire or talk to your boss about a raise, you are displaying a classic victim's mentality.

Nobody has known a child who fell off a few times while learning to walk, and then started crying and gave up. Children are great at being persistent until they make it happen. Whether it's learning to walk or drive, the principle doesn't change.

Our educational systems force us into being perfectionists, to be always right and do the right things – or get punished. From physical punishment in lower standards and mental punishments in higher standards – an individual develops a deep down fear of making mistakes.

"If you want to increase your success rate, double your failure rate," said Thomas Watson, founder of IBM.

The question is: are you smart enough to learn from your mistakes?

2. But I am just an innocent, little lad lost in the world.

Big and little have nothing to do in the real sense of the world. It's just a matter of perception and self-image. If you think you are little, you are. If you think you are big, you are right again. You will find instructions to boost your personal image in chapter 11.

3. Let's not upset (or anger) anyone.

A victim usually believes he or she has to be the most nicest and pleasing person of the world. This is a common belief enforced while upbringing by parents or authority figures such as teachers or relatives by saying things like, "Be nice", "Don't be a jerk", "We won't take you anywhere if you don't behave like a good boy/girl."

This habit is a killer, mind you and puts you directly under the control of others. Talk about a miserable life!

People will get upset if they feel they have the right to get upset. Don't give them this right. We are designed to respect those who respect themselves. Give yourself a chance to respect your priorities and time. Others will learn soon.

4. I don't want to hurt other's feelings

Everyone has the ability and power to take control of their emotions and feelings. We are all responsible for the way we choose to feel. You don't have to take care of them like a child and do things that massage their feelings. You are not hurting anyone, they are hurting themselves. We are all free to feel what we want to feel.

5. It's not fair; the World is not fair; what they do is not fair!

If everything in this world was fair, you and I would be sitting in our closets with our fair share in the world like everyone else. All the possibilities of the growth of this world and our personal self would be closed. We would come to a dead-end.

If you expect the world to be fair, you are probably forgetting an important fact that since the world actually isn't fair, you have the opportunity to go ahead and make your life exactly the way you want it to be. And there's nothing to stop you from doing so.

Do you know the 80/20 rule? It says that 80% of the world's money is in the hands of 20% of the world's entire population. Rest of the world has what's left out.

If you suffer from this syndrome, quit whining – go ahead and claim your share.

6. They'll think I'm stupid

If I was to tell you that those you fear think ill of you – are hiding in their own closets and shaking with fear for what you might be thinking about them, would you believe me?

Do you find it funny? This is what is actually happening in the real world.

What others think about you is actually none of your business anyway. If you are running around expecting people to think you're stupid (or actually asking them to see if what you said or did was stupid), you are putting yourself at the mercy of others.

You have the choice to keep your personal opinion about yourself – the sole opinion that matters. And it's worth making that choice.

7. I need someone to help me out every time and in everything.

Lack of self-belief often results in seeking help outside. Though it may be a good idea to take expert advice, you are the best judge for making decisions that run your life. Yet most people are running their lives as decided by others.

Getting others cooperation is essential for success. But depending more than required on others and especially when you are making key decisions of your life can easily backfire.

If you let others make decisions for you, you are going to have a very tough time living a fulfilled life.

In chapter 9, you will learn how to formulate your own goals and decide what you really want for yourself.

8. Success is reserved for others, not for me.

Why not you? When God created us, he created us alike. And if you are someone who'd like a more scientific explanation (like me), here it is.

The latest breakthrough in the world of human psychology has been responsible for revealing information that might just change the world. NLP – short for neuro-linguistic programming is a study of human excellence which has proven again and again that anything in this world which has been ever done, be it success or failure, can be copied. In fact, this is how our brains operate.

There are no if's and but's involved in this fact. It is a scientifically proven truth and when you follow the techniques given in this book, you will be able to prove this for yourself too. Keep doing the exercises and you'll know.

The Process of Victimisation

We are taught to be victims throughout our lives. Firstly, it's our parents who act as the dominating figures of our life, and persuade us into believing that the way to live the life is by proving yourself to others.

The way parents withold love whenever the child needs it, the most creates a deep sense of fear and a serious lack of self-confidence and self-esteem in the child's mind.

The greatest fear of a child is to be devoid of the love which he or she could get from the parents. By withdrawing that love, parents unknowingly condition their child into feelings which will lead into the development of a problematic personality, therefore, undermining his/her self-confidence and self-esteem.

Parents could be forceful about their child's career, their education, and actually make decisions on his part when the child could have been asked to make one. This is a common fallacy which forces the child into taking whatever is given to him. And this is what the child's mind gets, that it is only capable of receiving that much, and spends the rest of its life attracting and accepting just what comes its way. This makes him indecisive, enforces a poor self-image and then turns his entire life into a disaster.

How many people do you see every day that are stung by the victim's mentality? They are everywhere; it could be your neighbour or someone in your family. It could also be YOU.

Are you accepting something in your life which you could change if you just went ahead, took some solid action and turned it around?

If your answer is 'yes', you are victimising your own self. I don't feel very good saying this, but most often we are the greatest culprits when it comes to destroying our own self-confidence.

Remember. what I first said at the starting of this book? You have everything that you need to achieve anything in your life, be it success, or confidence, or anything. You just have to discover it inside you. It's all there.

When it's all inside there, what are you looking for outside? Guidance? It's good to seek guidance. But have you waited and carefully analysed whether the help you are getting is up to the mark or not?

Most people live their lives based on the decisions of others. 'You ought to become a doctor', 'You will become a highly ranked officer', 'You must score 90% marks this year".

Although rewards are good, but are you victimising yourself or letting yourself victimised if you are just accepting what others are deciding about you?

If you are in a job, are you letting others decide things for you? Is your boss taking a little too much extra benefit of your over-niceness?

Are your friends taking away your money from you because they know you are too nice to ask them your money back?

Gosh.

If that's so, give yourself a break.

The Confidence Killers – Guilt & Fear

Guilt

Guilt is one of those deadly emotions which can instantly kill confidence and destroy any chances of its development ever again, until it is recognised, dealt with and replaced with positive emotions.

Guilt is not a natural emotion. If you feel guilty for any of the actions which could bring you closer to your dreams, given that your dreams are positive and intend good for you and everybody else concerned, you are being victimised by this emotion.

For example, you could feel guilty for your sexual desires if bullied by the society and sometimes your parents to feel like so. Viewing the fact that sexual desire is a natural driving force, prevalent in each and every human being by nature to ensure replication of every living life on this earth, (and may be other planets too, who knows) any guilt for this desire is unnatural and outright wrong.

Of course, balance is crucial. Unmanaged sexual drive is as destructive as nuclear energy being used for destruction. I am talking about the good uses, not the negative ones.

Taking another example, you can easily find individuals who are literally victimised by their families to fulfil their responsibilities towards them, even the ones which have no base or use and are a complete waste of one's time and money.

You could feel guilty for things you should be doing for your family just because your family thinks so. The emotional attachment that drives this guilt makes it even worst. If you are facing this problem – understand this – they may be wrong in their thinking. Think about it seriously.

Believe it or not, many parents use guilt to control their children.

However, as effective as it always is, it leaves mental scars on the mind of the child which continues to berate his life forever.

Guilt is used by some people to control others in their daily lives. They do this either out of habit or by purpose by the virtue of their realisation that it is a highly effective controlling tool.

Guilt kills your confidence. You don't have to live with it and you mustn't if you intend to grow up into a healthy and mature adult with sufficient amounts of self-confidence and self-esteem.

From now onwards, start becoming aware of where and when you feel guilty for anything that could add good to your life. If you do, you have got something to deal with. An enemy discovered is an enemy half-whipped. Your awareness is sometimes enough to eliminate any negative emotional patterns. If not, you can go ahead and wipe them out using the techniques discussed later in this book.

Don't let anyone make you feel guilty for your natural desires and the right to be FREE and do whatever it is that you want to do. Purposely deflect every attempt to make you feel guilty. If you see someone trying to use it repeatedly on you even after your hidden warnings, you need to deal with that person in a little tougher way – you know what I mean.

Fear

Fear is the deadliest of all emotions and is responsible for destroying more dreams than anything else in this world.

A victim is fearful of many things in life and continues to be victimised by them forever. In most cases, fear becomes such an integral part of one's personality that it begins to govern each and every area of life.

We deal with fears, its causes and the solutions in chapter 6.

There Are Things You Cannot Change – Live With Them

For some people, this is really very hard to swallow.

There are things which you cannot change. It's as if some unseen force wants it to be just like that and in spite of your greatest efforts, you are helpless. There are things which you simply cannot alter.

Are you uncomfortable with this fact? Are you uncomfortable with the fact that you will eventually have to die? Are you uncomfortable with the fact that the world is not a very easy place to live in and with?

A classic victim's mentality is to whine about things which cannot be changed. You cannot change weather, yet you can find people who will let weather determine their moods. And since they know they cannot change it, they have something to whine about.

"Everybody talks about the weather
but nobody does anything about it."

—Mark Twain

The problem is that this kind of a habit – blaming outside conditions which seem to change your mood and the way you feel, is just a display of the victim's mentality. You are once again, letting others outside your direct influence control your life and hence your destiny.

Do you remember the definition of insanity we talked about earlier? It's doing the same things over and over again and expecting different results. Whining and complaining about things you cannot change is no different than this.

Once you learn to let go of the things which you cannot change and accept them wholeheartedly, you will begin to see a great difference in the way you view your life. Your way of seeing the world will also change. You will begin to see the greater things which you otherwise were missing because you were too busy noticing things which were out of your control.

"Grant me the serenity to accept the things I cannot change,
the courage to change the things I can,
and the wisdom to know the difference."

—Reinhold Niebuhr

Focusing on things we can change is a better way to deal with the life rather than pushing ourselves around about the things we cannot change.

Ask yourself about the things that you seem to whine about but cannot change.

There are only twenty-four hours in a day. Do you worry and

whine about having less time? Think about it, is it better to go ahead and learn the art of time management or moan about how short time is? Does it make any difference to time? I wish clocks could listen, but they can't. They aren't so wise. (Or maybe they are – that's why they are so quiet).

Quit Living in Your Past

Your past could be a matter of great pride and at the same time, a matter of great frustration for you. In fact, it could be easily the greatest roadblock in your path to a greater self-confidence and of course, success in life.

We are prone to living in our pasts. Most people believe that it's their past which determines their present and the future. In reality, past doesn't even exist except in their minds. Your present is exactly what you choose to live in the moment and your future shall depend on what you do today as well as in that particular moment when it shall arrive.

You could learn great lessons from the past and use them in your future life. But if your past is becoming an obstacle in your present and future success, you need to redefine its role in your life.

If you are living in the past, you are once again fulfilling the classic mentality of the victim, by blaming things that happened in the past to be certain that all present failures and problems are nothing but a result of their own past.

Some people never fail to astonish me. They take such great pride in their problems, frustrations and failures of their past to emphasise how great they are of having faced them. Unknowingly, they are only adding to their own remorse. They are pushing their minds into harmful habits of drawing negative energy from their past and in turn the mind is attracting more of it. It's a self-propagating, endless loop of inner frustration.

You will usually see these people struggling in some matter in their lives, usually which are finances, or relationships or their own health.

If you believe what happened in your past determines your present, and eventually your future, you are doing nothing but just exercising your own great power of making a choice when it comes to taking control of your own life. It's only that you have chosen yourself to be limited with regard to your past.

Your life shall give you many lessons and experiences. Your duty is to extract the best out of it, and use it to enhance your present and future. Blaming the conditions, circumstances, people and other things in your past to undermine your own future and present is like shooting at your own foot.

You are intelligent enough to know that YOU can choose not to come in your own way of success. You can do this, can't you?

What's out of your control, God has chosen to deal with it directly. Stop bothering about it.

4

THE GREATEST SECRET OF AN UNSHAKEABLE SELF-CONFIDENCE

"There are Universal Laws at work..."

—Wallace D. Wattles,

The Science of Getting Rich

On the eastern frontiers of France surge up the grand mountains of Alps, piercing the skies with their unimaginable heights, spread everywhere around and scaring even the mightiest of hearts with their invincible presence.

In the midst of incredible snow and ice, where even a slip of foot could vanish any living being forever, a man crossed these mountains with 60,000 of his men, each one of them loaded with food and weapons, a feat no one else had ever dared to think about before.

Napoleon Bonaparte – the name that reminds one of the greatest military commanders who ever walked upon this earth has many incredible feats to his name.

What is it about some people that they are able to take upon any challenge, any situation and turn it around to their advantage?

The way that these people turn around things in the period of greatest challenges, where a common human being will break down clearly, conveys that they know something which others don't – a secret which allows them to break through any obstacle in their way to accomplishment of their goals.

The greatest leaders in the history of the world possessed gigantic amounts of Self-Confidence. Napoleon Bonaparte was known to have such self-confidence that his presence alone filled his generals and soldiers with confidence and vigour.

Imagine what will happen if you were suddenly given the key to the source of this kind of self-confidence?

What if I told you that that source is already within you and you are using it right now? And that you have been using it for your entire life?

It's inside all of us at our service. And yet, it has been almost a secret for over countless centuries...

It is the secret that has created innumerable millionaires, great leaders and magnificent speakers...

It is what has created those men and women who rocked the world with their presence...

Get ready to be surprised...as the secret is so simple that you have probably been ignoring it all the time.

The secret is the **power of thought.**

The entire personal development industry is based on some very strong foundations, one of them being the power of a human being's thoughts to design a life full of choices and accomplish literally anything he or she wants.

The law operating behind all this process is called **'The Law of Attraction'.**

Before you begin to think that this is some new-age crap – **understand this:** Your personal belief about the power of thought doesn't affect its presence at all, just like the law of gravity cannot be denied by not believing in it.

The world has not yet known a man or woman who decided to stake everything they had for accomplishing their dream and failed permanently. These are the people who failed miserably again and again and still managed to achieve what they wanted so dearly. It was none other than their ability to control their thoughts and hence, maintain their focus on what they wanted, rather than the obstacles.

"If you advance confidently in the direction of your dreams,
and endeavour to live the life which you have imagined,
you will meet with a success unexpected in common hours."

—Henry David Thoreau

An unshakeable belief in one's own ability (remember the dictionary meaning of confidence?) is the factor working behind this kind of behaviour. And this ability comes from a deep understanding of the fact that we are the ultimate creators of our own lives, capable of doing things which we never think we can do generally.

I have heard of a woman who lifted a car when she saw her child crushed beneath its front tire. Amazed and bewildered, when people asked her to do it again, she said she couldn't and had no idea how she accomplished it.

Many other examples like these clearly demonstrate what a human being can accomplish when it simply decides to make something happen. All limitations die at that moment, the layers are suddenly broken and that hidden you appears from nowhere.

People from low profile backgrounds and with literally no financial backing have turned around things to build big empires and become financial giants. People with deformed bodies go ahead and take part in Olympics.

Roger Bannister broke the four-minute mile after it was declared impossible to be achieved by any human being, by top-notch scientists and physiologists of that time.

Henry Ford never went to college. Thomas Edison failed high school. Einstein was stamped as a fool by his math's teacher.

There's something that these men and women understood that an average man didn't (and still doesn't). It's the ingredient using which they climbed the ladders of mind-boggling success.

The Greatest Secret Revealed

Real self-confidence begins with the understanding that it's you who eventually controls everything that's going on in your life. Whatever it is that you want to be, do or have in your future lifetime totally depends on the type of thoughts you are going to choose and dwell upon. It has always been so and is always going to be...

If you think you CAN get successful, you WILL...

If you think you CAN write that best-selling book, you WILL...

If you think you CAN become financially free, you WILL...

If you think you CAN win that game, you WILL...

Just think about it...what is confidence? It's when you feel deep inside your heart and mind that you CAN...and you **go ahead** and make it happen. Even if you fail once, twice or thousand times and still you think you CAN, ultimately you WILL make it happen.

Thomas Edison, the great inventor, failed around 10,000 times while inventing light bulb. He eventually did it!

A reporter went ahead and asked Mr. Edison before he was about to reach his breakthrough invention and inquired if he was discouraged by so many failures. To this he replied, and this reply has become a classic, "I haven't failed, I have discovered 10,000 different ways by which I cannot make a light bulb".

Talk about super levels of self-confidence. This still blows my mind when I think about it. If you can develop this kind of attitude, your failure will become impossible.

Napoleon Bonaparte was indisputably one of the greatest leaders that ever walked upon the earth. During one of the many battles he fought, his soldiers began to catch a viral disease which spread quickly amongst his soldiers.

Upon watching a soldier being ruthlessly ignored by other soldiers because he had that disease, Napoleon himself walked and sat down beside him. Looking at the bewildered soldiers, he said, "Believe that you will be ill and nothing can stop you from getting it. It's all a matter of belief." As you must have guessed already, Napoleon never developed any illness.

It is this kind of confidence which creates outstanding successes. It all comes down to what we think and believe deep inside our minds which ultimately manifests and stands before us. It is not luck. It is not destiny. It's the physical result of your thoughts which kicked off the process of its manifestation. It's **your** creation.

Your Thoughts Have the Power to Become a Reality

"Reality is merely an illusion, albeit a very persistent one."

—Albert Einstein

It's your thoughts which have brought you **where** you are today, **what** you are today and what you **have** today.

You are **who** you are right now...and you are **where** you are right now... because of the total sum of the thoughts you've had to this point in your life.

Whatever it is you have been thinking about so far... is happening in your life. Your present is the result of your previous thinking....and your future will be the result of what you choose to think today!

You do have a choice, if you think about it. Thoughts are the only thing over which you have total control and fortunately for us, it is the thing which ultimately controls everything else in our lives.

In this book, you will receive some specific tools and techniques to take control of your thoughts and manage them in a masterful way. But for now, it's important that you begin to understand the greatest power that you already possess and can use to bring about any change in your life.

Think Your Way to Super-Confidence

You can easily find people who think and talk continuously about financial failures, financial problems and about their bad finances when what they actually want is **financial freedom.**

You can easily find many people who will argue with you for their own limitations and failures. If you have tried changing someone's mind towards the good things in life, you know what I am talking about here.

"Argue for your limitations, and they are surely yours."

— Richard Bach, *Illusions*

What you continuously think and dwell upon, manifests! It really is that simple?

You can compare your mind with a super computer which has amazing and really extraordinary features. Imagine buying such a computer to your home and discovering there's no instruction manual with it. What are you going to do with this computer, in spite of all its marvellous features?

We are all living with such amazing and powerful equipment in our heads. Unfortunately we don't come with an instruction manual.

Most of us aren't aware of what's going on in our minds all the time. Emotions that seem to have no feet and only wings continuously bewilder us. The human brain is a complex machine.

On the top of that, advertisers, marketers and people of influence who do understand the power of the human mind use it to further confuse us and persuade us to go their way. And most people go along because they do not know that they have been influenced by some subtle methods which their conscious mind failed to understand.

This is a very dangerous scenario. It means that any average human being can be persuaded to buy, eat and do things which are not good for health. And this is what is happening all around the world.

You see overweight, obese people whose minds have been conditioned into wrong habits of eating and are being continuously re-conditioned by the advertisers around the world.

You see politicians speaking **into** the minds of people, giving suggestions which lure them into believing what the speaker wants them to believe.

...that life is a struggle, ...that success is reserved for the lucky, ... that we humans are just tiny specks in the vast universe.... These are some beliefs which the majority of the world is living by.

We are consistently being **seduced** by the society's enforcement of false and dangerous beliefs and stigmas which have limited us into our shells. Most people are walking with their dreams hidden in their hearts, covered with layers and layers of false beliefs and limitations which the society has put there merely by repetition.

And the whole objective of these efforts is to initiate or stimulate *'thought'*, **the way THEY want it.**

Can you remember a time when you felt totally fresh and full of energy and had a few people tell you that you looked unwell or ill and you actually started feeling like that?

If you don't, I can bet that if two or three people told this to you in a row you would actually begin to feel that way. This is the power of suggestion at work. Most of us around the world have no idea that this is happening to us all the time.

No wonder life seems to be so difficult. With all this confusion and chaos around, what else it could be? What we choose to think and believe eventually becomes our reality. It's really that simple!

The Master Key to Self-Confidence

The reality that everything in your life has been happening by the virtue of your thoughts is the proof that you are already a powerful creator...

There's a small difference though. All this process of creation has so far been unconscious in nature. You have been manifesting things which you didn't realise.

It's time to change it all, once and forever! The first step is to ensure that you master your thought process **consciously** from now onwards.

You must think what you want to think...

You want to think abundance...

You want to think success...

You want to think prosperity...

You want to think confidence...

At first it's a little difficult, eh?

But then, like all other habits, it becomes easier day by day until you have mastered it.

In the same way you must start monitoring your thought process consciously from now onwards and making the required shifts to keep yourself in alignment with the way you want your life to be.

It is difficult if you only monitor your thoughts. Just imagine, a normal human being has over 60,000 thoughts running through his/her mind every day. Can you monitor them all?

Your mind would go crazy if you did that.

So here's the key...watch your **FEELINGS**. In any moment while you want to monitor your thought process, pay a close attention to what you are exactly feeling. Watch your feeling closely. Your feelings are a direct result of what you are thinking...and it's always an exact match.

"What you think, what you feel and what manifests is always an exact match."

—The Secret (2006 movie)

Do you **fear** that you will fail the interview you are going to take tomorrow morning? Well, you probably will. Fear is a feeling which is a result of your innermost negative thoughts.

Are you **afraid** of talking to the one you really like ...because you think you will be rejected? Behold... your feelings are most probably about to become a reality.

As a side note, think about it. Are you rejecting yourself before even giving the chance to the other person to reject you?

Living in our comfort zones, most people in this world choose to stay where they are. It's more comfortable. It's more pleasurable to stay there rather than taking the step into the unknown and face uncertain results.

On the flip side, if you choose to feel only joy, happiness, abundance and love....what do you think will begin to happen?

If you have understood the above concepts, you can easily imagine what happens when you worry. You are simply focusing on what you don't want and mixing it with intense emotions. Your subconscious which understands the language of emotions is receiving all these signals and is bringing you back the exact same thing which you are trying to get out of your life.

If I ask you not to think of the colour blue, what will you think?

Understand this: Your mind does not know the difference between what you want and what you don't want unless you specifically let it know by directing your focus.

If you are feeling like a victim, you are sending powerful instructions to your subconscious mind which takes them as command and brings back to you the physical equivalents.

Is it any wonder that the rich get richer and poor get poorer?

Now you know!

EXERCISE PRE-PREPARATION

As you sit back comfortably and begin to relax, imagine a person who has an unlimited, unshakeable self-confidence, standing in the middle of a crowd...such as a party or a gathering. Make this a 3-D picture. Think in detail.

Pay attention to the energy that person exudes. Look at the posture, the smile, the look in the eyes. Listen to his/her voice; how does it sound?

Seeing or meeting a confident person is always a wonderful experience. A super confident person exudes a positive, vibrating energy which seems to envelope in its aura everything and everyone around.

In the presence of a bright, confident person you feel your entire being uplifted. Your spirit goes high, motivation increases and a stream of positive thoughts runs down your mind. You begin to feel confident too.

A confident human being is a walking magnet and seems to attract everything he or she wants easily and comfortably.

Confident people seem to take upon any challenge, any difficulty and any obstacle and master it, no matter what. It's always the most confident person who is chosen or seen as the leader. It's the confident person who takes risks and becomes financially free and lives his life his own way. Presence of a confident person creates an aura of certainty and relaxes everyone around.

Confidence brings success...

Confidence brings happiness...

Confidence brings joy...

Confidence brings colour to life...

Confidence brings a meaning to the life...

Confidence brings literally everything you can ever imagine...

If only you have enough confidence, you can accomplish things others can only dream about....

Do you want to be the kind of person you just imagined above? Yes? Go ahead and replace the picture of that person with your own. See yourself standing in the previous picture with the same level of confidence you imagined....the same posture...look in your eyes and the smile on your face. See what you are wearing, how others are responding to you and the joy you seem to have inside you.

You are that person...Yes! **You** are that person!

Note: If you are having a trouble visualising, see Appendix A for help.

Exercise 1

Moving on, there must be someone whose confidence levels you admire a lot; a colleague, friend, someone in your family or even a famous personality who oozes self-confidence; someone who has high self-esteem and, therefore, you admire.

Think about this person if you would like your confidence levels to boost up just like him or her.

On the other hand, this is your chance to start from scratch – to improve the way you walk, talk, and think; and your body language on the whole. Choose a person you know who has the kind of confidence you want. It could be a person from history, a celebrity or someone you personally know.

Choose this person as your **Confidence Role Model.**

Think of this person, observe in your mind how he/she behaves in key situations of life and keep that overall image in your mind.

You have to now fill out the following sections. But make sure the person whose confidence levels you admire is really worth that admiration.

My Confidence Role Model

He/she would act like…
He/she would talk like…
He/she would walk like…
He/she would think like…
Their body language would be like…
Other people think that this person is…
When faced with problems, this person thinks…
When dealing with opposite sex, this person behaves….

Now take note of the few things you have written down about your confidence role model. Add them to your confidence list (the one you created in last chapter). The idea is to make an effort to be like you desire to be. So let's start with the basics.

Put these qualities into action.

Act as if you are the person you want to be and notice the results.

Don't worry if this feels awkward, because it will! After all you are acting out what you are really not. It will take a while for it to sink within and feel normal.

Perhaps the most fastest and powerful way to create change in you is to start believing that the change has **already** happened. If you start believing it as **already done**, your mind will go ahead and make it happen in the real world. Again, the power of thoughts is always at work. It will never fail you.

Try this in the real world by doing a simple exercise: Begin talking to a stranger while you behave and act as if that person was your childhood friend. Let your verbal and non-verbal communication completely display that you are talking to an old friend.

Then see what happens...

Installing the Qualities of an Unshakeable Confidence

This is an extension of the above exercise. What it does is that it takes the qualities you seek and installs them inside you automatically. Yeah, you read it right, it's automatic.

Sit back comfortably with no distractions. Put off the lights if they disturb you. Just make sure there's no interference.

Close your eyes and imagine a movie screen in front of you. Play a movie with your Confidence Role Model in action. Observe him/her going through life, acting confidently in various situations of life. Do this for 2-3 minutes.

Now, imagine yourself stepping forward and stand behind your role model. Take a step forward and enter into his/her body and then play the movie again. Only this time you pretend that you are that person. Go through all the motions again as above pretending to be that person. Do this for 2-3 minutes or until you are fully drenched into the powerful feelings.

Say to yourself, "As I count from 1 to 5, I will feel like I have never felt before; Confident, Magnetic and Powerful. I now possess all the qualities I seek from my role model."

Count from 1-5 and open your eyes.

Do this exercise everyday for the next 30 days.

Exercise 2

Write down your biggest confidence challenge. Describe in writing exactly what you feel when you encounter that challenge.

Now think about how your Confidence Role Model will behave in the situation you find the most challenging. Begin to act as if you had those abilities in that situation.

DO NOT skip any exercise! Each exercise is designed to help you influence your subconscious mind and create a lasting change. Stick with them and the results will astonish you!

5

THE BELIEFS OF CONFIDENCE

"There is no defeat except from within.
There's really no insurmountable barrier
save your own inherent weakness of purpose."

—Emerson

In my personal journey towards confidence, nothing has astonished me more than the incredible effect of beliefs on my life. And you are going to feel the same the moment you realise the power beliefs have on your life.

This discovery came gradually, when during my own journey towards a greater self-confidence I began to observe my habits, behaviours and feelings carefully. I was literally blown away by the way my hidden beliefs were controlling every area of my life and governing everything I EVER felt and experienced.

Beliefs are the governing factor in everything we do, be or have in our life. In fact, we experience only what our beliefs allow us.

"To accomplish great things, we must not only act,
but also dream; not only plan, but also believe."

—Anatole France

A belief is a command to your nervous system. When a belief is triggered in a situation, the whole nervous system follows this command without any question.

If you get nervous easily, you are holding beliefs which are commanding your nervous system to get into a nervous state.

Beliefs are not just thoughts – or dominating thoughts – they delve even deeper where your entire internal system nods in unison to its presence and purpose.

This is why beliefs are so powerful. And this is exactly why you MUST change the beliefs that hold you back.

Unless you go ahead and understand these beliefs consciously and weed out or replace what we do NOT want, you shall always keep on wondering why certain things happen in your life.

Why it is you who always fail in a particular situation, when everyone seems to do it right?

Why is it you who is unlucky?

Beliefs. Hidden Unconscious Beliefs.

Beliefs have the power to limit even the most talented person on the earth as well as push the most unintelligent and dull person to the heights of success.

It was belief that made Roger Bannister to break the four-minute mile (not that he was unintelligent – it's just an example), after it was rendered impossible by the scientists and physiologists around the world.

It was belief that made Napoleon Bonaparte rise to a supreme position in the French military and almost win the entire world at such a small age.

Just think of it, it's hard to run a country, imagine running the whole world. Most people can't even run their homes properly. Even then, there have been leaders and kings who managed to rule the world.

The greatest men and women who ever walked on earth had an unwavering belief in their ability to make a difference in the world. This is precisely why they could make a difference. Beliefs are the catalysts by which mind accelerates success. Nothing has been EVER achieved before it was believed that it could be done. All discoveries, all inventions and all new creations are a result of the belief which works at the back of all of it, pushing the mind to find new ways to make things happen.

Belief is everything. Having a set of powerful beliefs can literally skyrocket your success overnight. If you believe in your capabilities, in a particular area of your life or about life in general, you will easily overcome the obstacles which give others heartaches. Our entire personality is made of who we believe we are in our depths of mind. By changing your beliefs, you change your entire life.

If I didn't believe that I can write this book, you would never be reading it. I had to work myself up to the point where I felt for certain that I was fully ready and capable to help others find real self-confidence in themselves. This book has been delayed twice, in order to see where I stood in terms of self-confidence and on my own scale of confidence evaluation before I even started writing it.

Belief stimulates that part of your mind which knows to make things happen. And it just makes it happen.

A man got stuck inside a refrigerator while he was working in a cooling plant. At the end of the day, everything closed down and the man was left alone in the entire plant – trapped in the refrigerator.

To the sheer amazement of the workers who opened the plant the next morning, the man was found frozen inside that refrigerator – dead.

So what? you'd say. Anyone would freeze at temperature that goes way below 0 degree Celsius.

Actually, there was never any electricity. The refrigerator wasn't cooling at all. The man died because he **believed** that the refrigerator was going to freeze him to death. And he died, frozen by the power of his own mind.

Are you beginning to understand the amazing power of your beliefs? So far whoever you are is only because you have believed so much in your abilities.

If you are not confident, it's because you have a belief that you don't believe in yourself.

A belief can be compared to a coloured lens by which we see the world. Everyone has different beliefs and sees the world with a different coloured lens. This doesn't change the colour of the world and what it really is. It only changes the way you see it. This is called **perception.**

Have you ever found yourself changing your attitude towards a person you thought was bad and who turned out to be a totally cool person that you actually liked?

Think of the people who came from lowly backgrounds and ended up being in the histories of success. Think of Abraham Lincoln, Napoleon Bonaparte, and Mahatma Gandhi....

When you change a belief, the entire world seems to change with it. Because nothing in this life has any meaning except what you choose to give to it.

Your beliefs form your reality and hence, control your entire life. By expanding your belief system, you enhance your ability to see the world.

How Beliefs are Formed

Imagine a child hearing the same 'You can't do anything' and 'You are good for nothing' continuously by his parents as well as from the teachers. The statement 'You can't do anything' gets so ingrained in the mind of the child that by the time he grows up it begins to govern every other area of his life, besides studies.

And when he's forty and sees an opportunity to make something happen in his life, relationships, career or business... the old voice comes back, 'You can't do anything', 'You are good for nothing'.

In the same way, false beliefs about self and about other areas of our life become a part of your unconscious and begin to govern all areas of your life. They are formed due to influences like dominating people in our life, from society and other sources like television or advertisements.

Usually these beliefs are so deep-rooted in our subconscious that they control our entire life by virtue of their presence. You won't even know why you get extremely nervous, throat choked and full of sweat when you are about to appear in an interview (or in any other key situation).

It might be due to an old situation when you became a target of everybody's laughter. Or may be a past humiliation you received for a behaviour someone you considered dominating.

Your mind very carefully registers these situations and makes a point to avoid these conditions in the future.

In short, we run away from everything that gives pain and run towards what keeps us in the boundaries of pleasure. In his book, *Awaken the Giant Within*, Anthony Robbins refers to Pain & Pleasure as the two forces which shape our life. According to him, we human beings are continuously striving to avoid what gives us pain and run towards what gives us pleasure.

The key, therefore, is to change the way you connect pain and pleasure to the things you want to change. We'll look at these strategies later in this chapter.

How is a Belief Strengthened?

A belief is strengthened by the help of references. It's like a never ending loop. You could receive a comment on your ability to sing or dance beautifully (or anything else) and your mind will register it immediately.

Next time you are about to sing or dance (whatever it is), your mind will generate the memory of you receiving a compliment and you will give another good performance. And then you receive more compliments which your mind continues to register.

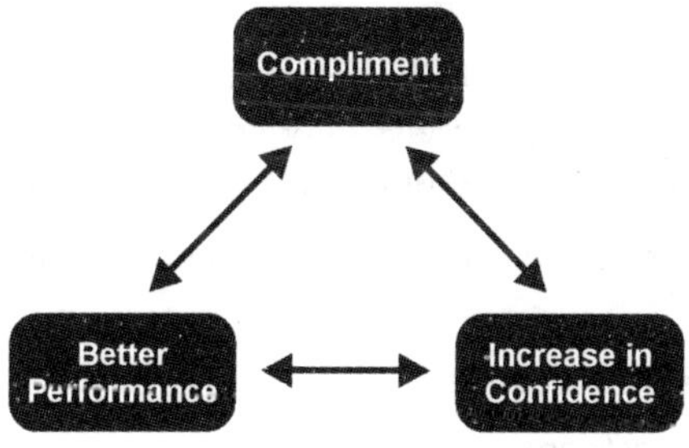

It's like a never-ending loop.

Similarly,

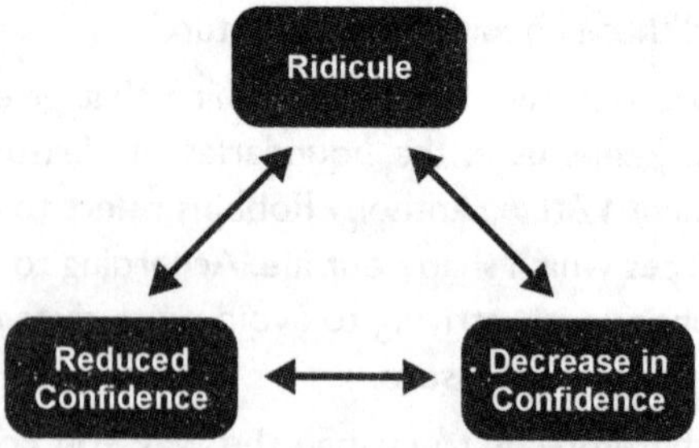

The same happens with your beliefs. With enough references, and more experiences based on those references, your beliefs continue to strengthen until they become a natural part of your personality. Beliefs like these stay in your subconscious and govern your entire life and continue that loop of more experiences and more references forever, until they are consciously recognised and manipulated.

Using the right tools and techniques which you will receive in this chapter, you will be able to recognise and change your beliefs forever.

How to Develop a Strong Belief System?

There are simple questions you can ask yourself to begin, to clarify and develop a strong inner belief system, so that you can make decisions that are right for you.

Having a strong value/inner belief system is very much dependent on our ability to accept ourselves – who we are, what we feel, how we see the world independent of what others say, think, feel and do.

The benefits of a strong inner belief system are varied and great:

- Stronger self-confidence
- Healthy self-esteem
- Greater life satisfaction
- Comfort with self and others

But how exactly does one go about developing this strong inner belief system?

Here are some questions for you to consider.

Finding the answers to these can help you begin to weed out the muck of "everybody else says," and get back to the purity and perfection of self-expression.

1. What are your current beliefs about work, life, people, and about yourself? Let us go and try a free-writing exercise.

On top of a page write one word (work, life, etc; one for each page) and then free associate for each word.

Write down whatever thoughts might be conjured up by the word at the top of the page.

Write until each page is full!

2. How much of what you believe is your own?

Take a look at what you wrote on each page.

What messages may have come from parents, friends, family, peers, teachers, etc?

Identify the recurring themes?

Now, pick out and highlight the things you feel truly reflect who you are and what you believe.

3. How much of it is enabling versus disabling?

Are the messages that came from others enabling and empowering? Or are they limiting?

Now, look at the ones that reflect your own inner belief system – are those empowering or limiting?

How do they make you feel?

4. What do you want to believe?

Mull over your true beliefs.

Do they reflect how you want to feel about life, work, people and yourself?

Write each idea or thought down on the left hand side of a page, and on the right hand side, write how you'd like to feel/think about each instead.

Reprogramme yourself by identifying these limiting thoughts as they pop into your head, and replacing them with the thoughts and ideas you identified on the right hand side instead.

If you continue this exercise, you'll find the old limiting thoughts creeping up less and less, and the new empowering thoughts will begin to take their place.

5. What messages about life, people, work and yourself did you get from family as you shaped your personality?

Be prepared.

Messages from family members are repetitive and will keep coming up.

If you have chosen to reprogramme any of their thoughts, values and beliefs, then be prepared to counter these beliefs whenever a family member articulates them.

6. What's your response when you express your belief and someone disagrees?

How are you going to respond should you share your beliefs with others, and find that they disagree?

Here's a hint: don't change your mind. It's OK that someone else believes differently from you–that's what makes the world go round after all.

Instead, simply state that you see life/work/people etc. differently, and then repeat and reconfirm your belief to yourself.

These questions, their answers and the exercises associated with each are sure to strengthen your belief system. Just like your soul that gives you life, you don't have to reinforce or communicate your belief. Nevertheless, its presence is undisputed.

As you explore your answers to these questions, and explore the exercises associated with each, you'll begin to realise that you do have a very strong belief system.

You may not always enforce or communicate it, but it's there, just as your spirit and soul gives you life.

The hard part then, is in developing confidence in your ability to express, in an unwavering fashion, these beliefs.

There are sure to be people who will disregard your beliefs. What you have to do is test your ability to continue with your belief system and keep it intact as a part of your personal growth. If it continues to feel solid, then restate and reinforce it strongly.

Moving ahead, in the process, once your belief system has been strengthened, you will find that those having less confidence in their own beliefs will seek you out.

It's a beautiful discovery, trust me. When you know you have the ability to help others, you begin to strengthen your belief in yourself even more. By helping others achieve more Self-confidence; your own confidence will continue to develop forever at rapid speeds, for the rest of your life. Once you have identified your beliefs, you are now ready to change them for good.

Question Your Old Beliefs

Just like a drop of poison can infect an entire well full of clean, drinking water, questioning your beliefs can have almost the same effect on your beliefs.

When you question a belief, you sow a seed of doubt.

Shakespeare once said, "Our doubts are traitors and make us lose the good we oft might win by fearing to attempt."

Even the most self-confident people can become a victim of doubt. And once a doubt creeps its way in, it can distort belief and destroy it.

That is why you must resolutely keep yourself away from the company which tends to sow doubts in your positive, well-serving and powerful beliefs.

However, we will use this particular model of distortion for destroying our old negative beliefs which harm our purpose of succeeding in life using...

The Magical and Almost Mind-Blowing Art of REFRAMING

Reframing is a process through which you can smash your entire belief system in a matter of just a few minutes.

The term 'Reframing' comes from Neuro-Linguistic Programming (NLP) which provides an almost magical way of turning your beliefs around, play with them, mould them just the way you want them to be and replace them with the ones you want!

Basically, reframing works on the concept of questioning your old negative beliefs and replaces them with new empowering beliefs.

People having tremendous levels of self-confidence are those who keep on reframing their reactions, thoughts and beliefs to and about particular situations all the time. It's an unconscious process for them.

Your car stuck in traffic? Are you feeling angry or happy? May be it's time to listen to your favourite CD you weren't able to get time to listen. You could reframe this situation and view it as an opportunity to think about the things you are grateful for in your life. You may want to visualise your goals or rehearse a future situation to make it just the way you want it to be.

There are countless ways of reacting to a situation. Basically, this is exactly what reframing gives to you. It provides you with tools using which you can observe a situation from many possible angles, like a director choosing the best angle for his scene.

You already know the power beliefs have over our entire life. Imagine the power you'll have when you know how to reframe your beliefs in a small time. And why you and only you will also have the ability to take someone's belief system and literally change it within a few minutes.

Talk about changing **realities**. Yes, you read it right. When you change beliefs, you change realities.

(1) Begin by asking yourself, "What is this belief based upon?"

Is it based upon a fact I know – or is it an assumption – or is it based upon something which isn't concrete and solid enough?"

Continue with the following questions:

1. Could there be a rational reason backing up this belief? Or there is none?
2. Could I be mistaken about this belief?
3. If I can be mistaken about it, why am I allowing it to run my life?

(2) Tear your old beliefs apart

Most of the beliefs are simply generalisations. It's a property of our mind to generalise things for future ease and to avoid the process of re-learning.

Just imagine if you had to learn to drive every day before you went to work. (Funny, eh?)

However, when it comes down to beliefs, this property of mind can create belief systems which are totally out of proportion and plainly harmful.

"Politicians are bad". Now that's just a plain statement – a belief with no reference to how, what, who, where or why.

"I'm a loser." Ahh… Now this is a powerful generalisation which massively impacts an individual's life and literally distorts everything. Just imagine how absurd it is to know that it is just a generalisation of one or two small failures, often followed by negative comments from others and hence, forming a belief which strengthened day by day. And it happens to all of us every day. Come on, it happens to **you** and me too.

Get Specific. Tearing your belief apart makes it lose its power upon you dramatically. Just get into the details and watch the belief melting in front of your eyes.

Remember the section on the power of Questions? In order to break through your negative beliefs, we'll access this powerful and magnificent resource.

What is the cause of this belief?
How specifically is it so?
What has to happen in order for me to not believe it anymore?
Am I willing to make that happen?
How specifically can I go ahead and make it happen?

(3) Apply your belief to someone else's life.

If you see someone else in a similar situation as you are in, would you believe the same about that person too?

Recently a female friend of mine got into an argument about the role of men and women in the growth of the world with a gentleman. I had the opportunity to closely watch them spill their guts. It was fun, actually.

The gentleman out of nowhere replied to one of my friend's comment with "Women are the weaker sex. They are weaker than men, physically and that really matters. Physical power commands more respect".

I had not been expecting the answer my friend came up with almost instantly. The answer shocked me as well as the other person.

"Does that mean that if you are physically weaker than anyone in this world, you don't deserve his respect?"

It was a killer – a complete turnaround that pushed the gentleman off-guard. You can imagine the look on his face at that moment. I was completely amused.

What my friend unknowingly was able to accomplish was to deflect a 'belief' that gentleman had with a question that made him doubt his belief – instantly.

You can do the same with your beliefs. So if you have a belief of the sort – "Since I can't speak well on the stage, I am a loser". Or "I must be a loser because I am unable to attract that particular person."

Just turn it around and apply it to someone else's life. Choose someone you respect and admire as it usually helps. Or just globalise it (as in the first example of my friend).

So for the above belief, ask yourself, "Does that mean if anyone in this world (or a particular person you respect and admire) can't accomplish that (the particular action or a result) in a particular situation (or lack a particular skill), that makes him a loser?"

It's really a killer. And it happens to be my favourite way of deflecting any negative beliefs I personally encounter.

You can use the above methods to deflect any negative belief somebody tries to force upon you. Just bombard the other person with your power questions and see him crumbling. It's like having an anti-negative-belief ninja's sabre in your hands – slashing your opponents.

Guess what, you can do it with anyone's beliefs. Just make sure you practice enough first and always do this to others with good intentions. What you do to others comes back doubled – it's a law.

Be a saviour, if you have to.

6

MASTER YOUR INNER COMMUNICATION

"Be confident" was all he said while I stood beside him with my heart racing like a station wagon, my eyes popping out of their sockets and my legs trembling like an old car running at 100 miles per hour.

I went ahead telling myself it'd be OK. "It's going to be OK. Nothing will happen." I had to believe in him. He was after all, the lady killer of the college. At least that's what we used to call him. No one could ever understand how he could get any girl he wanted.

It felt like I was about to do something I was not meant to do. "This is not who I am. I can't do this" were the words shouting in my mind. And as I got closer, the intensity of the voice increased. I was frozen in my tracks.

In front of my eyes, I saw the girl I had admired for 3 years go away. I was too afraid to approach her and tell her what I had in my heart.

I felt like a loser. "She has better choices than you", something inside my mind whispered again.

Of course, I didn't like it that way. But I was helpless.

And I gave up…it was easy to crawl back into my shell.

Have you ever had anything like that happen to you?

I have not yet understood the meaning of the words, 'Be Confident'. I am sure you've heard them too. They are as hollow as a drained pumpkin. If they were enough, you wouldn't see most of the world locked up into its comfort zone, not even trying to get out of it, EVER.

Nor would there be any need for this book to be written.

Your inner voice – the communication that goes on in your mind – is generated from your innermost thoughts. And the impact that this voice has on you is mind-blowing.

Thought is the beginning of everything. Before this earth and even this universe existed, there was thought. The same principle applies in your life – your thoughts engage the magic of the universe. Everything you are today is the result of your previous thoughts and everything you will ever be, do or have depends on what you are thinking today.

So what are you thinking today? What's going on in your mind right now?

Your first step towards a life of total confidence and hence success is mastery of your inner thought process.

Let's talk a little bit about negative thoughts…

Olympian John Konrads won one gold and one bronze medal in the 1960 Rome Olympics. During the 400-metre freestyle, for which Konrads won the bronze medal, he said he lost focus by nurturing negative thoughts on how arch rival Murray was going to perform. Konrads confessed that though he had convinced himself he could win, these thoughts got in the way and blew his chances.

Actually, negative thoughts are commonplace and anyone can be a 'victim' to them. However, it's not the presence of negative thoughts but the way we handle and react to them that either breaks or makes our confidence and self-esteem.

Think over this:

Nothing has any meaning in life, except for the meaning you give to it.

Keep these things in your mind as we move on with this chapter:

- It's not only you that gets negative thoughts; everyone on this planet gets them.
- You are not making an attempt to uproot negative thoughts here. Just handling them more smartly.
- Negative thoughts, as such, do not harm you. It's what you say to yourself after the thought has entered your head that harms you.

- You can change any thought you want by changing what it means to you.

Analysing Your Thoughts

In this chapter, I want you to go deep into your own mind and find out what triggers off those negative thoughts and emotions you have about yourself.

FACT: It is not the trigger or the event that kicks off the bad feelings. What makes you feel despondent are the internal dialogues you say to yourself in response to the trigger. These catalysts distort reality and put your feelings in turmoil.

That's the kind of turmoil Lynette got into. Her husband Roger had been quite distracted over the past few days. Lynette tried talking to him on a couple of occasions but he wasn't forthcoming. She heard him talking in hushed tones over the phone, and he also came home late more often than before. Lynette was troubled beyond words. She spent hours talking to herself, wondering what Roger was up to.

Now she has two choices....

Either she can think:

- **"He's ignoring me."**
- **"Maybe he's having an affair with someone."**
- **"He doesn't find me attractive or interesting anymore."**

And trigger these emotions....

- **Anger**
- **Resentment**
- **Grief**
- **Self-pity**

Maybe she should have been more probing; or given more time to her husband. Did she know her husband well enough to arrive at these conclusions?

In fact Roger must have been having a tough time at work. A bad review by the boss, a fall in profits in business, tiff with a colleague. It could have been anything! The point is nothing in life has any meaning, only the meaning you give it.

Roger must have had a completely unconnected problem, but to Lynette it looked like a problem in their relationship!

Controlling your inner voice and what you say to yourself either makes or breaks your self-esteem and confidence.

Within this session, you will be introduced to a technique, which you can use to control your inner dialogue and to make you appraise just how hard and unreasonable you are on yourself.

But before we get into the exercise, let's just discuss those negative thoughts you have.

Here's a small little recap – It is not the trigger or the event that kicks off the bad feelings. But the internal dialogues you say to yourself in response to the trigger that makes you despondent.

Okay, to make it easier to understand, let's split these negative thoughts or distortions into 13 categories.

Here's the list. You can use this as a quick reference:

1. **Assuming**
2. **Over-generalising**
3. **'Shoulds'**
4. **Labelling**
5. **Binning the positives**
6. **And they all lived happily ever after**
7. **Blaming other people and events**
8. **It's all or nothing!**
9. **Negative thinking erodes your soul!**
10. **Believing what you feel**
11. **Personalising**
12. **Making comparisons with others**
13. **I can't cope with life**

While we go through them one by one, make note of the ones you use most frequently.

1. Assuming

When you make assumptions with your thinking, you are assuming the worst without knowing the full picture or without testing the evidence.

Let's go back to our example about Lynette and her husband. She didn't have any of the facts; she just assumed that her relationship with her husband was in deep trouble.

She could have tested the assumption by going up to him and saying "Roger, did I do something that upset you? What's wrong? I think we should talk this out."

Other examples of assuming self-talk are:

- **"I know this project is going to be rubbish"**
- **"I know I'll make loads of mistakes if I'm best man"**
- **"I know people will just hate me"**

How could you rephrase some of these thoughts above to make them more realistic? Example – "I am going to give this project a chance and make up my own mind."

2. Over-generalising

This is when you over-generalise your thoughts and make them more intense by the words you use.

For instance, you would say things like:

- "I always end up on the losing side."
- "I make mistakes in everything I do."
- "Everyone hates me."
- "Everyone thinks I am so dumb."
- "I never do any good at cooking."

Even when you read these lines their demoralising effect is so evident!

As much as you know that such over-generalising internal dialogues are inaccurate, unjust and unfair and affect your confidence, yet you use them.

You certainly are not making mistakes in everything you do!

C'mon! You think you are making a mistake right now?

Rubbish! It's not everything that you do then, is it?

How do you turn this around?

Well, a better phrase to use would be, **"Sometimes my cooking doesn't turn out very well but overall I am a good cook."**

Sounds fair? Look for the good in situations and what is working well. It can do wonders!

3. 'Shoulds'

Some people surround themselves with 'shoulds'.

- **"I should be thinner."**
- **"I should have more friends."**
- **"I should be earning more money."**

Are you the kind who says 'should' all the time?

'Shoulds' are the demands you place on yourself.

A 'should' represents what you are not doing but you think you should be!

So when you know you 'should' be doing something but are not doing it, how do you feel?

Inadequate, hopeless, frustrated? Yes, the list can go on.

So, what are your plans to get rid of the 'shoulds'?

It's easy. Just change the 'should' to 'want' or 'could'.

- **"I want to do this"**
- **"How could I do this?"**

4. Labelling

How often do you use an adjective to describe yourself?

Labelling is a common syndrome. This is when you give yourself a name or statement that describes who you are.

For example:

- **"I am a loser."**
- **"I am stupid."**
- **"I am ugly."**
- **"I am fat."**

How is it possible that you are a loser in every aspect of your life? Is there nothing in you that is attractive? Are you forever a dimwit? Of course not!

Stop labelling yourself and be specific in your thoughts. Instead of saying "I am a loser" say "That didn't work out how I would have liked."

5. Binning the positives

Do you tend to overlook the compliments people give you?

Do you refuse to accept and ignore if someone says "That was a great job, well done"

or "You look fantastic today"?

How do you usually reply to praise?

"Oh, it was nothing, it was easy" or "I don't look great really, you're just saying that."

Do you realise that you've just discounted the fact that you worked really hard to get that job done or that you took time over your appearance to get it right?

Let's set this record straight. A simple "Thank you" with a smile is the perfect response.

Think it over. Is it that much of an effort?

You would give credit to someone who did a great job. Make sure you accept the credit when you do a great job or when you receive a compliment.

6. And they all lived happily ever after

Perfection is an illusion.

Oh yes it is. No point arguing here.

So if you are a person who has to have everything perfect in your life, it's going to be pretty tough, buddy! You are setting yourself up for disappointments.

Do you have thoughts like:

- **"That shouldn't happen to me."**
- **"I can't believe that has happened."**
- **"That's unfair."**

Stop looking for that perfect world. Everyone has things happen to him or her, good and bad. You are not a special case and no one is exempt.

Instead accept that bad times fall on all and ask yourself "What could I do to improve this situation now?"

7. Blaming other people and events

Do you blame others and don't accept responsibility for outcomes that are different from your expectations?

Do you say?

- **"If only my parents had been more ambitious I'd have had more success by now."**
- **"If only I didn't have to impress all of the time."**
- **"He makes me feel so bad."**
- **"She had a hold over me which means I can't do anything."**

While this attitude is awful, it will also make you feel like a 'victim'. Forever you will move ahead with a sense of helplessness; that you are capable of nothing.

It isn't your fault. Is it?

YES, IT IS!

Agreed, the event has had an effect on you but at the end of the day only you have the responsibility to let it affect you.

So, how do you turn these thoughts around?

You can start by first focusing on the reality.

If you feel something is unfair or unjust, accept that it is. Think about it.

"If world was completely fair, YOU and I would be receiving our share of the world with all possibilities of succeeding any more closed down. And since the world ISN'T FAIR, we can use it, mould it and turn it around anyway we want".

Here's what to do: Accept that the impact it has on you is your responsibility.

Don't make excuses; it is your responsibility!

8. It's all or nothing!

There's more than just black and white. There are several colours in between, right? Like blue, green, red, yellow, pink, brown, purple, mauve...phew!

Then why are most aspects of life just black or white? Are you one of those who think "It's all or nothing"?

Are there no grey areas in between?!

- **"I am either a success or a failure."**
- **"If I get first place, I am a winner. If I get second place, I am a loser", irrespective if there are 20,000 runners!**
- **"If I don't get things 100% perfect, I am a flop."**
- **"If I don't get an A Grade in Math, I am a failure."**

Well, in life there are rarely successes and failures. In fact, success is a journey, not a destination.

Success and failures are not meant to be measured on a 100 or 0 scale. At the end of the day if you don't perform to your highest standards, it certainly doesn't mean you scored a zero!

Your "It's all or nothing" thought is only setting you up for failures.

How many times do you perform with absolute perfection?

Less than 10% of the time!

So, does that mean you are a failure 90% of the time? Now you know that's utter nonsense. Why should you always have to be perfect?

9. Negative thinking erodes your soul!

How do you react to events that don't work out the way you planned?

Negatively?

For instance, your boss has said that you completed a piece of work incorrectly, so you say to your partner that you have had a terrible day.

You may have burnt the pie, so the whole meal is ruined.

You might have cut your finger while hiking so the entire holiday is messed up.

Your thought makes the entire situation negative.

What happens if you change your focus when you start thinking negatively?

You can say:

- **"What is still good about this situation?"**
- **"That is only one bad thing, what are the good things?"**
- **"What could I still enjoy about this experience?"**

10. Believing what you feel

Feelings are not facts. If you believe your feelings blindly, too bad, my friend. Mend your ways or you are sure to suffer a confidence setback.

The quality of your life is based on your feelings.Feelings are only thoughts that we have decided to generate. That doesn't make them real.

You give meaning to your thoughts; and hence your feelings.

So, are you the type of person who believes all the feelings you have?

- **"I feel bad. Therefore, I must be bad."**
- **"I feel like a loser. Therefore, I must be a loser."**
- **"I feel ugly. Therefore, I must be ugly."**

Low levels of confidence can distort your thoughts. So you really need to question your feelings before you believe them.

Ask yourself questions like:

- **"What would someone who is a 100% loser, be like, bad or ugly?"**
- **"Am I really like that?"**

Challenge your feelings by questioning them.

11. Personalising

Personalising is when you blame yourself. It happens when you say:

- **"It's entirely my fault that my son didn't get the chances in life."**
- **"If I wasn't so clingy, men would stay with me."**
- **"It's all my fault that we got divorced."**

Blaming yourself for other's actions and decision means you are taking too many responsibilities on your shoulders. Don't!

Simply because you are not accountable for someone else's decision-making.

Remember that you are not the only one giving advice or offering opinions. An individual meets numerous people and hence gets a number of opinions. But in the end he or she has the freedom to decide what he or she wants to do.

Agreed mistakes do happen and some of them could be the result of your action or decision. But all of them? You don't believe that, do you?

Your confidence is suffering a blow every time you hold yourself liable for someone else's life turning out to be miserable.

Take the reins of your life into your hands. Don't blame yourself and don't let others do it unjustly.

12. Making comparisons with others

This has already been discussed before, but for a reminder –

Do you always compare yourself to others? If you do, it's high time you stop. Why are you putting yourself through so much of worthless competition? Frankly, it isn't even healthy competition.

What you are doing through such a comparison is that you magnify your 'weaknesses' and others' 'strengths' or shrink others' 'weaknesses' and your 'strengths'.

So, are you saying something like this?

- **"I haven't got a chance for this job, after all who is going to want to hire a single Mum? Maria is young, single and she has got a degree."**
- **"I am hopeless at spelling and math, Mark is great at these, he can do them standing on his head."**
- **"No one will want to go out with me, I've got a big nose. Look at Donna. She is beautiful, has lovely hair and really nice skin."**

Challenge these thoughts! Appreciate that you are a unique person and stop these distortions.

13. I can't cope with life

If you find yourself saying stuff like:

- **"I can't stand it."**
- **"I couldn't live without you."**
- **"I can manage this."**

So what are you doing? Accepting defeat and telling yourself that you are not strong enough to cope with life?

Yes, a lot of things in life are unpleasant, difficult and not nice. But you can cope with it! A better way of saying something is:

"I don't really like this but I can stand it."

How do you challenge and question this thinking? By asking the following:

- **"If this does happen, will I really be helpless and be unable to cope?"**
- **"If the worst happens, what will I do?"**
- **"When I look back in 30 years time, will anyone really care about this?"**

How to Overcome Negative Comments from Others

Nothing has any meaning in life except the meaning YOU give to it.

You've heard that before, haven't you? How far have you come to believe in it?

It's not what people say to you that is a problem. People talk! Yes, they do, and there is nothing you can do to stop them. However, it's what you say to yourself after people say something unpleasant that leads to a problem.

Are you left behind with a feeling of dejection?

Let's tackle that feeling, and banish it from your life once and forever!

Responding Effectively to Confidence Destroyers

Like we discussed a few seconds ago that people talk and it's hardly possible to stop them. In such a case, how do you respond to negative comments coming from others with or without an intention to make you feel miserable about yourself?

For instance, when Candace wore a new bold pink dress to office, her colleague Syrah said, "Yikes! That's way too bright Candace." With her nose up in the air, Syrah ranted on, "I would never wear something like that."

What do you think Candace would have said?

"Eh... Yeah... I did think it was too bright. Maybe I shouldn't have worn it. Why did I even buy it?"

But Candace did not sulk or curse herself.

In fact, this is what she said, and please note, with a twinkle in her eyes:

"I know Syrah, this colour is really bold. But you know what; it makes me feel bright and happy. Maybe I could spread some of my vivacity to others around me. What say you?"

You bet Syrah was quite taken aback. And you know what, a couple of weeks later, she might have bought herself a dress of the same colour!

Candace didn't stop wearing bright-coloured clothes. She could carry them off and was comfortable in depicting a vibrant personality. She believed in what she did.

Doesn't this incident agree with the adage – No one can make you feel inferior without your consent?

It's not what people say to you that affects your confidence. It's what you say to yourself after they've stopped talking that either makes or breaks your self-esteem. It's all about self-communication and it is directly under your control.

Every feeling tells you something, but you should learn to take them with a pinch of salt.

Remember it has been made up by what you have been thinking and saying to yourself.

It will take time to learn them all, but build up gradually and you will start to build up your confidence.

Here are a few feelings and thoughts that you are sure to face sometime or the other. Check what kind of action you can practice in such a case.

FEELING: "I don't feel confident about the way I look"

ACTION: Improve your overall appearance. Would losing or putting on (in case you are painfully thin) some weight make you feel great? If so DO IT! What clothes would your Confidence Role Model wear to feel good? Get a new haircut and treat yourself to some new clothes – it always makes you feel better and more confident. Buy something new each month and when you put it on, view it as your own confidence booster.

FEELING: "I'm afraid of that person – I'm never confident around him/her"

ACTION: Just remember, they eat, sleep, go to the toilet just like you do and mostly they have the same problems as you - they just don't show it! Think – How would your Confidence Role Model deal with this person? What would they do?

Remember that confidence is about acting – they are just better actors than you right now. Think of the things you can do that they can't do – how would they feel if the roles were reversed? Getting any closer?

FEELING: "I'm afraid of the feedback and reaction I'm going to get when I complete this piece of work"

ACTION: Hey, as long as you've done everything to the best of your ability, you don't have to worry. And if you do make a mistake or two, what the heck? Just learn from them for next time. A person who never makes mistakes is not doing anything. Those people who moan and groan about things always seem to do nothing. There are no failures in life as long as you learn from the outcome. You're a winner!

FEELING: "I'm really worried about this..."

ACTION: Time to usher in your Confidence Role Model again (when did you ever let her/him go, right?). Would my Confidence Role Model worry about this? How would they deal with this situation? What would they do? In the grand scheme of things what will worrying do to this problem? Is there any action I can take to fix this right now?

FEELING: "My friends are really negative thinkers and this just festers onto me when I'm with them"

ACTION: Don't get rid of your friends but make sure you surround yourself with positive and progressive people also. Surround yourself with people who are like your role model.

You know what your friends are like beforehand, so just accept them for what they are. If they are true friends just acknowledge that they are who they are and you are who you are.

FEELING: "I can't do this"

ACTION: Oh yes you can! Break the problem down into small chunks and attack each chunk separately. Nothing is ever as daunting as it first seems. How would your Confidence Role Model do this? Think of a time where you have done something really difficult – think this through in your mind and play it over and over like a video recording before you do the task in hand.

FEELING: "I've never got enough money to do the things that I want"

ACTION: Ask yourself what you are doing about it? Do you have "more month left at the end of the money" rather than "more money left at the end of the month" problem? Do you plan your budget? Do you know where all your money goes? If you answered yes to the first question and no to the next two, it's time you made a plan of action. For all you know, you may need another career to achieve the lifestyle you want?

FEELING: "I don't feel worthwhile as a person"

ACTION: Put down your strengths on a piece of paper. Don't forget to list down all your achievements in life from your exams, to when you passed your driving test, to the job interviews you cleared etc. Remind yourself that you've already had loads of successes and don't feel so sorry for yourself. After all, no matter where you are in life, there is always someone who is worse off than you. Put things into perspective; ask yourself what your Role Model would do.

More Actions

We are not done yet, so pick up a fresh piece of paper.

Write down all those confidence destroying statements that you say to yourself or others say to you. Now, write down what you are going to replace these thoughts with after the statements are made.

Write down next to each statement, why it is downright twaddle.

Confidence Sapping Friends & Colleagues

The people whom you hang out with, that is, family, friends or colleagues, they will have either a positive or negative effect on your levels of self-esteem and confidence.

You are sure to have been around people who are positive, happy and pleasant.

They are the ones who make you feel a welcome sight any day, who smile sincerely, and who encourage you rather than rain you down with advices and reprieves.

How do they make you feel?

Their personality rubs on to you too, making you feel positive, happy and pleasant. Such lively people can easily sprinkle zest into a boring atmosphere and can fill a room with constructive energy and upbeat vibes.

You must be familiar with the moaners too.

They are always putting people down, they don't like others being successful, they are jealous and are negative thinkers. Phew! That's a long list and it sure can go on.

Such people bleed dry your energy, bring down your energy levels and in a way take you a million miles away from the level you really want to be operating on. They try and urge you to join their team – a team of non-achievers.

Family members can be grumblers a lot of times, but you can always choose your friends; you can never choose your family!

So what should you do to make sure that the people you hang out with empower and support what you stand for rather than bring you down all of the time?

1. You have the power to choose who you hang out with. Ideally, you want happy, vibrant and positive people. Say, people who are more like Candace and less like Syrah.
2. If you have good friends who are negative and yet you want to hang around them, make a point of letting them know how you feel - if they are true friends, they will respect you for this. If they are negative from time to time, just acknowledge that this is what they are like and block out the negativity.
3. The same can be applied to family. Your older family members have behaviours that have been conditioned for years. Appreciate where they have come from and as stated before, select and extract the information that filters through to your brain. Be VERY selective in what you choose to put in your mind.
4. And remember to keep this statement in your minds always – Nothing has meaning in life except the meaning you give to it.

EXERCISES

The Free Writing Exercise

This is a very powerful exercise which will help you become extremely aware of your self-talk patterns.

Basically, this exercise helps you find out the contents of your unstoppable mental chatter that keeps on torturing you.

Here's what to do:

1. Take a few sheet of paper and a pen/pencil. You will throw these papers in the end so choose scrap paper if possible.
2. You are supposed to jot down everything that is going on in your mind.
3. Begin to write non-stop. Write as if you were on fire and writing would extinguish it. Don't think, don't edit. Just write for at least 15 minutes straight.
4. Write even the most irrelevant thoughts that come to your mind. Do not bother or judge if they are positive or negative. Just write non-stop.

5. Take a break. Go for a stroll for 5-10 minutes, drink some water. Do anything to change your mood. Just remember to come back.
6. Read carefully what you have written. Identify the negative themes carefully. Notice the consistent patterns which are appearing.
7. Now tear these papers and throw them away. This is a very important step. This is a powerful signal to your mind that no one else will read your thoughts which makes it comfortable.

Do this exercise everyday for the next 21 days. Notice the consistent thought patterns, especially the negative ones. The more you become aware of them, the more you will automatically begin to resist them and change them until they are completely gone.

The Power of Questions

Write down the answer to the following question:

Give me five reasons why you think you are a dumb head?

I am serious. Just write them down. Trust me on this one.

If you have a trouble coming up with the answers, I want you to persist until you have actually found five reasons. Go back to the store house of your brain, re-imagine your old experiences, tickle your brain cells a little and come up with five reasons.

Really, do it. OK. I hope you are done with the above (If not, please do it NOW).

Now write down five reasons to why you believe you are one of the smartest persons in the world?

Now persist again until you have found five solid reasons. Once again, sit in your imaginary super-jet, plunge yourself into your old memories and come up with five reasons. **Take as much time as you want.**

Done? Great!!!

Now pay attention to your answers. Were you able to write answers to all of them?

Your answer is probably yes. I know that because I am aware of one of the greatest principles of human mind. Any question that your mind encounters, it is compelled to and has the unquestionable ability and the power to ANSWER it. It doesn't matter if it has to make an answer up to quench your thirst for the information you are seeking through your question. It just does it.

That's how powerful your mind is.

Now pay attention, what questions are you asking yourself at a daily basis?

Are Your Questions Directing Your Focus in The Direction That You Want?

FACT: The process of questioning and answering is all the time going on inside your mind. All your thoughts, feelings and behaviours are the result of what questions you are asking your mind at daily basis and as a matter of routine, thereby determining your focus and hence your quality of life.

Your quality of life depends entirely upon what questions you ask to yourself. And so does your SELF-CONFIDENCE...

Want to hear a self-banter?

Here we go...

Why am I such a geek?

Why am I such a failure?

Why do I always fail?

Why am I so unlucky?

Why am I an idiot?

What did I do to deserve this?

FACT: Your mind is completely able and powerful to answer all these questions, even if it has to make them up.

Try asking this question to yourself, **"What are the things that I am extremely grateful for in my life?"**

Spend at least 5 minutes counting the things which you are grateful for. I am sure you can find many of them. It may be your family, your job, your body.... Go ahead and do it now.

Done?

Now tell me, did answering this question change your focus? Do you feel a fresh stream of thoughts and feelings rushing inside your mind and body?

Just imagine if you knew inside yourself that you have the ability to attract any one you want, what kind of questions would you be asking yourself?

They might be,

"How can I enjoy this process?"

"What can I learn from this?"

"How much fun am I going to have with this?"

Upon facing a setback, rejection or a temporary failure:

"How can I do this better next time?"

"What can I learn from this?"

So why not help out Bob ask some good questions? Let's go...

"How much fun this can be?" (Focusing on fun, joy... PLEASURE)

"What can I learn from this?" (Focusing on learning so that he can do better next time...PLEASURE)

"Is she worth my attention and approval? Is she worth all the mental, emotional and physical investment I am going to make in her?"

The last question results in setting a frame of total self-confidence and self-worth. In this frame, Bob's mind is now already evaluating and judging the girl he's about to approach and calculating his priorities. Hence, his entire mindset changes as a result. He is now in control and his feelings confirm the same.

If you pay attention to the above questions, the possibilities of any failure have been completely eliminated.

In this powerful frame, there are only results, no successes or failures.

Imagine the power you can have when you begin to consciously change your questions. Not only your self-confidence but your entire life begins to improve as a result of this new way of communicating in your inner world.

Now imagine what is possible when Bob combines the power of questions with all the other strategies given in this book.

Bob will become unstoppable!

Now I am going to give you a set of questions which you can ask yourself at a consistent basis consciously. Ask them to yourself until they have become a part of your unconscious process and begin to fire them automatically.

Here are the questions…

What am I most grateful for in my life?

What am I most excited about in my life?

How can I do this better?

What can I learn from this?

What are my greatest strengths?

Why is the world such a great place to be in?

What is the greatest thing about being alive?

What can I do better than anyone else?

What is my purpose on this earth?

How can I turn things around in my favour?

What choices/options do I have in this situation?

How fast and efficient can I have this work done?

How can I enjoy doing this work?

What is the greatest thing about this situation?

Let me give you a personal example. Writing a book wasn't a very easy task, at least at first. Nevertheless, I still wanted to write.

There were times when I was totally exhausted and my time-table required me to write at least a set number of pages….

It was then when the power of questions came to be of amazing assistance.

I consistently asked myself the following question:

"How can I enjoy this process?"

My mind always came up with at least two-three answers which actually enabled me to write this book. At the same time, while I was writing this book, I consistently asked myself, "How can I add a great value to my reader? What is the best way to write this which will benefit my reader the most?"

And to be honest, writing this book has been a tremendously positive experience for me. It's been fun and learning at the same time.

A Whole New Level

Let's take this to a whole new level. Just begin to ask yourself questions to things you don't have in your life. Ask these questions consistently and get ready to be amazed!

Here we go…

- **Why am I such a great communicator?**
- Why do women find me so irresistible? Why can't they keep their hands off me? (Turn it around if you are a woman)
- **Why can I crack any interview I want?**
- How blessed am I?

  BAM!!! Are you already beginning to see where it's going?
- **How powerful am I?**
- Why can I succeed in any calling of my life?
- **How well can I accomplish this?**

OK, it's exercise time. Put on your Exercise Spacesuit and get ready (and if you don't have any, just take a pen and paper.

Write down five questions which you believe harm your self-confidence and belittle the quality of your life.

Once you are done, turn these questions around into positive questions which you can now ask yourself at consistent basis.

An example would be, "Why am I a failure?" becomes "How can I succeed dramatically in my life?"

Very soon you will reach unconscious competence where the new way of asking questions will become a permanent habit.

Now you have this tool which can change your entire life and fill you with an unlimited self-confidence in a very little time. Go ahead and use it to change your life.

Whew, that was a long chapter. I sincerely hope that you learned a lot from it. Keep coming back to this chapter and review it again and again. It's only with practice and repetition that it will become a part of who you are.

7

THE SILENT LANGUAGE OF CONFIDENCE

Your career is about to take off. It's the interview you have been waiting for so long. And you are absolutely prepared. **It's the big day.**

You know deep inside you that you are going to overwhelm and literally wow the person across the desk with your amazing accomplishments.

Or you're ready to give the presentation you've prepared hard for months, the one that will make your career soar to new heights.

Or you're about to approach someone you like and admire for a long time and today you are all fired up to go ahead and just 'say it'.

Well, even before you have opened your mouth to utter even a single word, your body language has already spoken for you in volumes – and your body language may be 'saying' something entirely different.

Have you ever stopped and paid attention to what your body language conveys?

FACT: According to the Wall Street Journal Executive Career Site, non-verbal communication has far more influence than the verbal communication. Studies have found that body language makes up 55 per cent of the force of any given response, your voice tone, which includes sighs, pauses and modulation, accounts for exactly 38 per cent, and verbal communication provide a mere 7 per cent of the total communication.

That means a staggering 93 per cent of the entire communication is done on a non-verbal level!

Have you ever seen someone giving a presentation or a speech while her body language clearly betrays the words she speaks?

Has that ever happened to you?

Similarly, it's pitiful to see a guy working frantically on the words to say to the girl he likes and bothering least about the body language that is going to accompany it.

Here's a fact that literally blew my mind when I learned it. It says that almost the entire sexual communication happens at a non-verbal level and that we are genetically programmed to attract the opposite sex by virtue of our body language alone.

Think about it, if there were no words, no languages and no verbal way of communicating at all, how would you express your interest in someone you are sexually attracted to? You know it.

In almost every area of your life, it matters less what you say. It's how you say it that makes all the difference. You will hear this again and again in this chapter.

Does your body language convey confidence, competence and charisma? Or does it convey insecurity, lack of confidence and low energy?

Now, I am not saying that words aren't important at all. Mastery of words can lead you into amazing success in many areas of your life. But words alone won't get you anywhere.

Body language is the ultimate key to developing an unshakeable self-confidence. And the good news is, you can easily learn it.

The Language of Honesty

Body language is your inner self on an open display. This inner self consists of your subconscious beliefs, values and hidden intentions. While words can be faked, your gestures, facial expressions, hand motions, inflections in voice tone and other non-verbal cues can easily give away what you actually think and feel inside. If you stand or sit slouched or slumped, taking up a small space and not making much eye contact with the world around you, you are sending a clear, powerful signal to everyone out there.

"Stay away from me. I'm a loser. I don't deserve respect and attention."

This is by the way, a classic 'victim' posture.

Compare this to a person who carries himself with grace, projects a positive energy and deep calmness, holds his head high, makes a powerful eye contact with others and takes up a lot of space (a sign of self-comfort). It's a wonderful sight to see a person who exudes such confidence.

If you've seen a James Bond movie, you know what I am talking about. Watch his posture when he walks, sits, talks and do anything. His body language is decisive and deliberate. His entire body projects an unrestrained and unlimited self- confidence. (By the way, he is my favourite super-hero)

If you have seen someone having a remarkable body language, it's almost never by chance. A confident and notable body language is a result of conditioned mind-body habits.

Think about this when you see a military person the next time.

What you think and feel inside about yourself and the world will show up in the way you act and behave, **always!**

Not only this – it will have an immediate effect on your own state of mind and invariably effect your body language. I have learned to keep my thoughts only of a positive nature after I realised that I was unknowingly creating **powerful tension clots** in my body by thinking continual negative thoughts.

You are probably carrying these clots in your body as well. Notice that right now. Where in your body do you feel tension at this moment? Notice those places carefully. These are the places where your negative thoughts manifest their first presence. Ever heard someone complaining all the time about a headache? Ask them to watch what they are thinking continuously.

Negative thoughts restrict the flow of life-energy in your body and make it feel full of stress and tension. If you have ever been in a key situation of your life and you're your body wasn't in your control – understand that your thoughts were making it so.

It's incredible that how our quiet, innermost thoughts have an enormous effect in the way we feel and present ourselves to the outer world.

Similarly, thoughts of positive nature also affect your body powerfully. Positive thinkers exude confidence naturally because their body language reflects the calmness and power that comes from their inner thoughts.

Are you beginning to notice how every element discussed in this book connects to each other and invariably governs how you feel, act and behave? It is the synergetic effect of all these elements that create an unstoppable self-confidence.

Body language is not just about sitting and standing in a particular way which can charm the outside world and especially the opposite sex. It's your inner world on display.

We are **always** communicating something to the world in one or the other way. We cannot **not** communicate.

If your body language is closed and you are not making eye contact, you are communicating to the world: "I want to be alone. Don't bother me." And amazingly enough, nobody will actually bother you.

If you see someone who is willing to fight, his body language will give away all the signals.

The point is that at unconscious levels, we all understand these non-verbal signals.

So whether you are a man or woman, your enhanced physical presence will bestow you with great confidence and fill you with power and energy.

Physiology & Emotions

Your body language has powerful effects in the way you feel. You can use this fact to feel confident **any** time you want and in **any** situation.

Generally, what you feel inside will reflect in your body language. In order to change your body language all you need is to change your feelings. Go back to a time when you received some good news.

Most probably, your entire body language changed and became more open, a smile filled your face and eyes became brighter, all in a matter of a few seconds.

You can also use it the other way around. If you are feeling sad or depressed, start smiling. Yes, that crazy, stupid ear-to-ear smile will make it impossible for you to feel sad or depressed. Try it now, even if you have to force and see your emotions change in an instant.

If you are feeling tired and low on energy, do this. Stand up and take a few deep breaths, put a big smile on your face and start jumping. You could accompany this with some yelling and shouting like a kid does and then see what happens.

Yeah, do it alone unless you are with friends who'd love to accompany you. I recommend that you find such friends.

Compare this to the following situation. You are feeling really tired after a whole day's work and you receive a phone call from a friend who wants to invite you on a game you like or a party. Does your tiredness disappear in a flash? I bet it does.

OK, here's one more. Make a fist out of your hand and raise it to your face level. Clench your teeth and shout, **"Yes".**

How do you feel? Motivated? Energised? Confident?

Understand this: The way you use your body language has a powerful effect in the way you feel. You can use it to your advantage anytime and anywhere.

If you encounter a situation where you'd like to feel confident but cannot, notice your body language carefully. Observe the cues which are making you project a low confidence.

Now take a few deep breaths, stand straighter with your chest out and chin up, loosen up your arms and throw them on sides. Smile a little and take up more space, whether you are sitting or standing. Continue breathing slowly and deeply.

Do this for a few seconds and see your confidence rising and becoming evident.

Using Your Body to Your Advantage

From now onwards, you must begin to become aware of your body language consistently. Reprogramming your body language takes time and subtlety.

Before you walk through a doorway, pause and become aware of your body language. Are you slumping? Are you frowning? Change it right there. Proper breathing is the key. Take a few slow and deep breaths. Relax yourself physically and mentally.

Breathing has a tremendous effect on your body language and voice tone. If you make it a habit to breathe deeply all the time, it will become almost impossible for you to feel less than confident, sad or depressed. If you breathe properly all the time, you will never feel anxious, impatient or out of control.

Here's a body language chart you can use to your advantage. It compares the body language cues of a positive and negative body language.

As you go through your life, notice how and when you project negative body language cues. Change them consciously. Soon your new behaviours will become a part of who you really are.

Confident Body Language

- Leaning forward, eye contact, hand gestures: Sincerity, confidence, interest
- Natural tone, volume, pitch and pace of voice: Secure, confidence
- Strong eye contact: Openness and honesty
- Laughing fully without restrains: Secure, comfortable with self and others
- Changing facial expressions to accompany what is being said (smiling when being friendly, amusing look when surprised etc.): Secure self-esteem
- Feet on desk, hands behind head: Confident, dominant or superior
- Steepling: Dominance, authority

- Relaxed upright posture, arms swinging naturally while walking: Confident, slow, calculated and deliberate movements: Inner Confidence, self-assurance, power
- Strong, firm handshake: Confidence, security

Negative Body Language

- Leaning back and looking down: Lack of confidence, aloof
- Limp, weak handshake: Nervousness
- Leaning in too close: Could be threatening
- Weak, soft voice: Nervousness
- Clearing throat, saying "um, uh," using overly complex sentences: Insecurity, nervousness
- Dropping head and looking down: Untrustworthy
- Staring at other person during silences: Increases tension
- Maintaining eye contact too long (over 7-10 seconds): May cause anxiety or discomfort
- Rigid, stooped posture, feet shuffling: Lack of confidence
- Twiddling thumbs, drumming fingers: Not paying attention, anxiety
- Clenching or wringing hands, playing with jewellery, sitting on edge of chair, jiggling foot: Stress, nervousness, anxiety
- Touching your face: Nervousness, dishonesty

Body Language at Work

There is a considerable and clear difference between the body language of a CEO of a company and a regular employee. And so is the level of respect they command.

However, you don't have to become a CEO to be respected like one. The way you carry yourself will make others unconsciously determine the level of respect you deserve and they will feel compelled to do so.

Your success in life depends a lot on how well you carry yourself. If you want to be something, you've to carry yourself the exact way that 'something' would. You must create what is called a 'commanding presence', if you want to be taken seriously in your life.

An experienced teacher usually knows how to use his presence alone to put a class to silence. An inexperienced teacher could miserably fail at doing this. Your ability to take up space without tension, walking gracefully and yet confidently and speaking with a clear and natural tone of voice are some cues that command a strong presence.

If you are involved in consulting business, a commanding presence can put your clients to ease. It is a clear signal that you know your business. It can create trust more rapidly than a hundred reasons you would give them to trust you. However, sometimes you might need to soften your presence when you need to empathise with your client. This is usually the case in personal consulting business.

If you are a teacher, speaker, trainer or a coach, and you want to be taken seriously (who doesn't want that?), you need to work extra harder to polish your physical presence. People follow those that they respect, fear and trust them. Your commanding presence accomplishes it all.

The key is to generate power through your physical presence. And there are certain techniques which can help you into doing so.

Body Language in Relationships

Even in your relationships, body language can have undeniable and sometimes irreversible effects, whether positive or negative.

Once again, what you say isn't that important. It's **how** you say that matters. Saying "I love you" to your partner when your body and eyes speak the exact opposite can backfire. If relationship was a person, this would equal to stabbing him.

"Our non-verbal messages often contradict what we say in words," says Jo-Ann Vega, president of JV Career and Human Resources Consulting Services in Nyack, N.Y. "When we send mixed messages or our verbal messages don't jibe with our body statements, our credibility can crumble because most smart interviewers believe the non-verbal."

So, now here are a few powerful techniques to use your body language to display an unshakeable and unstoppable self-confidence:

- Never look at the floor (down) when you walk (look above horizon).
- Keep your hands out of your pockets.
- Breathe deeply and slowly throughout the day.
- Stick out your chest.
- Shoulders up but relaxed.
- When you walk, walk slowly, bigger steps, but slow. Use the technique given later in this chapter to improve your walk, if you think it sucks.
- Use lot of space no matter where you are.
- Don't dress in too many dark colours.
- Don't be afraid to go into people's personal space. Just make sure you don't make them too uncomfortable by jumping in directly. Make it a gradual process. This is a sign of confidence.
- Lean back.
- Avoid closing your arms in front of your chest. (unless you're feeling cold).
- If you are talking on phone, stand up and your tone will become more decisive.

Unleash the Magic of Your Voice

Have you ever found yourself mesmerised with the voice of a tele-caller or customer care executive? Or...

Have you felt attracted to the voice of someone only to find out later to your disappointment that the person was plain looking? And amazingly enough, you still find yourself attracted?

Your voice tone is an incredibly powerful tool you can leverage upon to easily influence others and make a powerful presence anywhere and anytime.

Having a rich timbre instantly boosts your own self-confidence and helps communicate directly to other's subconscious minds, making an instant impact. It makes you more attractive, more powerful, more commanding and unimaginably influential. Use it to your own best advantage.

Most people sound like they had something stuck in their throat. It's annoying to hear such a voice.

A powerful body language must invariably be accompanied by a powerful voice tone in order to project maximum congruency. You don't want to be someone with a great body language and a meek voice tone.

In order to sound like a pro, you must keep a regular check on the way you sound to others. You have probably heard the voice tone of voice artists who speak in advertisements. Just imagine, these people are paid only for the quality of their voice because their voice not only raises the overall quality of ad but also communicates powerfully to the viewer's unconscious minds, something which every company wants to make happen.

Over the phone, your voice tone is the only way to project maximum impression on your listener.

It doesn't matter if you want to get paid for your voice or not – in order to become more confident, start becoming aware of your voice from now onwards. Here are a few techniques to make your voice mesmerising. Practice them everyday until your new voice tone has become a permanent habit.

Like any other habit, your mind and body both must work together to depict a great tone.

(1) The tone of your voice follows your **state of mind**. If you are excited, your voice naturally depicts excitement. If you are feeling angry, your tone will change to express your anger. Similarly, if you are relaxed, you will naturally speak more comfortably and give your voice maximum room to project itself.

If you are nervous, your voice will become weak and feeble. When you are feeling confident, your voice will automatically adjust itself to display that confidence.

The first step is to keep your mind in control using the techniques discussed in the chapter on mastering your inner voice.

(2) **Always breathe deeply** and from your diaphragm. Avoid shallow breathing altogether. The way you breathe has an instant impact on the way you sound to others.

Similarly, avoid speaking from your nose or throat. Speak from your chest and if possible, even deeper (it is possible). Notice carefully if you are speaking through your nose? It's very irritating for your listeners.

Place your hand on your chest and speak, **"This is my chest".** Notice the difference. If you do it right, your chest muscles should vibrate. You can do the same by placing your hand on your throat and nose to see how you sound when you speak from there.

(3) **Drink lots of water** to keep your vocal cords lubricated. This is especially important when you making a presentation or a speech. Professional speakers always make sure that they have plenty of water every day.

(4) **Record your voice**. Most people have never heard their voice from a third-person's perspective. When you will record your voice and hear it later, you will be astonished at the apparent difference. The point is that even if you think that you sound good, it may not be true.

While you practice these techniques, record your voice at small intervals, like a week and notice the changes.

(5) **Ask others.** Chances are that you will be amazed at the feedback you receive.

Here's another secret – A good tonality can secretly spark attraction for you in the mind of your listener. If you have ever met someone who is really good with the opposite sex, you must have noticed his or her voice tone as deep and really pleasing.

Your voice tone can turn your partner on, if you use it right. Use it to your advantage.

Dressing Up For Confidence

Your dressing sense forms a very significant part of your body language.

The way you dress up has two immediate effects:

1. It governs the way you feel.
2. It governs the way others feel about you.

If you are someone who doesn't really care much about dressing properly, it screams out a clear, crisp and loud message to the world.

"I have low self-esteem and self-worth. Do NOT respect me."

No. You don't need to dress like a rock star. I am talking about clothes that suit one's personality, are clean and well pressed. Also, it's not about costly clothes. There are many places where genuine and good quality clothes can be bought without burning your pocket.

Anyone can choose to dress like that. Still, most people don't even spend a little amount of time to understand what looks good on them.

One Sunday morning, a few months ago, I went to pay my mobile bill at a nearby outlet. It was a holiday and I was not really in a mood to get ready properly. So I just got up and went there with my shorts and slippers on. The bill was somewhat larger than the usual cash I keep with me. So I handed a cheque that I had already brought with me to the lady sitting on the cash counter. With a look you would give to someone you believe is an idiot, the cashier looked at me up and down and said,

"Do you have sufficient amount in your bank account?"

What a shocker!

I said 'Yes' meekly, feeling both funny and embarrassed. I swear I have never been that careless ever again.

Imagine that happening with a man who goes for an interview with unclean or messed up clothes and then complains about how he couldn't get selected in spite of the fact that everything went right.

While I am sure you aren't one of them, but just in case you are, change it immediately. Learn a little bit about fashion, trends etc. It doesn't matter what your age is, it is never late to learn.

I know parents who wouldn't ask their children what looks good on them. Children are generally more fashion savvy these days. What's the harm in asking?

If you are a guy, find a girl who you think knows about fashion. Most of them do. Girls are eager to jump at the idea of shopping. Just ask her to go out on shopping with you and let her pick you some clothes. (Ask her to come along with you and have fun shopping, not 'HELP' you out. You don't need help, you just need advice. In this way, she'll have more fun.)

If you are a woman, just ask your girl friends who are fashion savvy. They can help you out better than anybody else. I have seen girls who literally transformed to something any man will fall in love with by just changing the way they dress and apply the right make-up.

Here's a rule of thumb for clothes: Spend more and buy less. Focus on quality not quantity.

The same rule goes for hygiene. If your nails are not cut, your hair going out of control, your teeth dirty or your shoes not properly clean, you don't really have an excuse for assassinating your own presence. I won't say much in this since I assume that you are already intelligent enough to understand it.

If you are concerned about it, take advice from a close friend or someone you know who really cares for you (not someone who just wants to please you). It's hard to listen to someone blurt out negative things about you but it's worth every miniscule of effort.

Pay **very** careful attention to your hygiene. It matters more than most people believe.

The Confident Walk

The following technique comes from **Kevin Hogan,** a master of persuasion and mind power. His teachings have had an incredible effect on the way I see and present myself to the world.

This technique tells you how to improve your own walking style for projecting maximum and powerful physical presence.

When you walk, imagine a hand pushing at your butt. Make sure your body is relaxed. Watch out for any tensions in your body.

Try this once and notice the results. Use this for a few days and it will become a permanent habit.

I personally used to walk with a big swagger and always received unwelcome comments for the way I walked. I tried everything to improve my walk – even some of the most expensive body language courses available online but none of them have had a more powerful impact on my walk as this single technique. It's so simple and yet so effective.

Not only this technique improves your walk – it makes you appear more confident and powerful by adding stability to your body language and making it seem more decisive and dominant.

Try it, it works!

Now, taking it a step further, always walk deliberately without any unnecessary movements, shifting or fidgeting your body. Move in a controlled fashion (not like a robot) to make others instantly perceive as powerful and super confident.

When you stand or sit, do not fidget with your hands or any other body part. Stand and sit calmly with minimal movements of your body. The key is to be totally relaxed as if you have all the time in the world.

Even in professional meetings, keep your body relaxed and your movements deliberate while your eyes display complete alertness.

8

MASTER YOUR SEXUAL SELF

Confidence is an indirect result of various factors working in synergy. Perhaps one of the most important factors is your ability to channel your sexual energy into various areas of your life which produces what is called '**Sexual Confidence'.**

In his classic book, *Think and Grow Rich*, Napoleon Hill, probably the greatest researcher on success and wealth-creation in the 21st century has devoted an entire chapter to the process of Sex transmutation, which explains how to use one's sexual energy by channelling it into different areas of your life.

However, in this chapter, I am going to give you a different take on this topic – How it applies to your Self-Confidence?

When I talk about 'Sexual Confidence', 'Sexuality' or 'Sexual Energy', they have nothing to do with sex, contrary to the popular belief. These terms have a much greater role in our lives than simply sexual intercourse.

What is Sexual Confidence?

Sexual confidence, first of all is not having a great body nor it's about knowing how to talk sexually or sensually. It's not about these things at all.

Sexual confidence means being able to recognise precisely what you like and dislike when it comes to your own sexual desires, and be able to express it confidently. That may mean exploring your own body to find out what pleases you.

Sexual confidence is not age dependent. Your being 50, 60 or above doesn't affect your sexual confidence.

Some older men and women find themselves more sexual confident than they were in their own teenage and younger age. Christina, 39, says, "If I was as sexually confident as today when I was 23, I would have not missed the amount of fun and fulfilment I could have had."

Sexual confidence is your ability to accept and express your own sexuality and being totally comfortable and cool about it.

If you're sexually insecure or uptight, or you feel as if you aren't very good at it, you are lacking in sexual confidence.

If you feel uncomfortable around the opposite sex, find yourself nervous and feel incapable to express your sexual interest, you need to work on your sexual confidence.

A man who isn't afraid to express his sexuality and has a high amount of sexual confidence is perceived by women as sexy. Women are very intuitive at determining how confident a man is just by watching his body language.

The same is true for women. A woman who has a high sexual confidence can in spite of her looks attract a worthy man. A woman with low sexual confidence, however, doesn't matter how beautiful she is will be uptight with her sexuality, tense during sex and would be unable to discover her true sexual potential.

Your sexual confidence directly depends on two factors:

1. Your awareness and comfort with your own sexuality.
2. Your ability to manage your sexual energy.

Sexuality

Sexuality is your individual inclination towards your sexual preference. It's a completely personal affair. However, the society's views about sexuality are based upon many old thoughts and ideas that have changed with times. Yet, the old beliefs still govern our lives and hinder us from expressing our sexuality comfortably. We do this both consciously and unconsciously.

Especially where religion is concerned, sexuality has always been in conflict. How comfortable are you with your own sexuality?

We have been taught since early childhood and throughout our upbringing that we should be ashamed, fearful and guilty for our sexual desires. It is also taught that it is against God's wishes for us to embrace our individual sexuality.

Discovering and understanding your own sexual desires and inclinations is perfectly normal.

Understand this: The whole universe is based on the principle of replication. (Go find some books on physics or read books by Stephen Hawkins). Sex, which is a medium of replication on earth, is the greatest form of stimulation available to man.

By determining your own likes and dislikes and your sexual preferences and by being able to comfortably express them, you will develop high amounts of sexual confidence.

Note: The point of my argument is not about going against society and thinking and behaving senselessly when it comes to sex. It's about discovering your own preferences, desires and being comfortable with them.

Erotic Energy

The myriad ways sexual energy directly or indirectly affects the various elements of our personality has never failed to astonish me.

Sexual energy is the erotic energy of your being. It's natural and exists inside everyone and expresses itself through your entire being. A good amount of sexual energy when properly channelled and understood can help you attain many great benefits.

Some of these benefits are:

- Attracting opposite sex.
- Creating an upbeat, magnetic personality.
- To be able to sell, argue and communicate with precision, clarity and confidence.
- Animate and empower your body language and hence your presence.
- Naturally make people like you for who you are and the energy you radiate.

- Achieving great health and vitality by virtue of the healing powers of the sexual energy.

All these factors combine to form the backbone of the tools and techniques which you are going to learn and have been learning in this entire book. If you are lacking sexual energy, your body and mind will refuse to work in a synergistic combination and shall produce a state of mind where you might:

- want to avoid social situations, thereby closing all possibilities of development of a healthy self-confidence.
- develop a fearful personality.
- feel a constant lack of energy.
- develop a shaky, unstable and insecure personality.
- physical and mental weakness; lack of concentration.
- reduction of will power; inability to handle challenging situations of life.
- lack of motivation to go after your goals and;
- repel the opposite sex.

In a state of low sexual energy, your entire mind and body may respond negatively whenever you are about to meet and interact someone of the opposite sex and is instantly picked up by the other person.

This is particular true for men, as women are naturally intuitive of catching sexual energy in a man and respond in unconscious ways. Most of the attraction that a man creates in a woman is not because of his looks, way of talking or any other characteristic but from a deep inner reservoir of sexual energy which women are very good at noticing and getting attracted to.

A man or a woman with good amounts of sexual energy naturally begins to develop the necessary characteristics which are required to attract the opposite sex.

If you have heard a woman say, "There's something about him that attracts me deeply but I am not sure what exactly it is", you now know what she means when she mentions this 'something'.

I know men who are so concerned about the way they look that they completely overlook the actually important details. Looks matter but only to the extent that they can help you begin with. In reality, any worthy woman (in terms of looks, intelligence etc) will prefer to remain with a man who is comfortable with his sexuality and has a secure, powerful and masculine presence, even if he doesn't score much in the looks department.

Sexual stimulation is probably the most important and powerful stimulations that a human being can ever experience. The emotion of sex is the supreme emotion which can motivate any man or woman into achieving great heights of success. It's of great amazement that almost all the men and women who have ever been truly successful, and those who are getting successful in life are those with highly sexed natures, whether they show it or not.

Sexual energy affects all your activities of daily life, your inner communication, your outer communication with people and the world, your levels of motivation, zeal, enthusiasm, energy and the ability to break through fears and overcome obstacles.

Your sexual energy affects your determination to achieve any goals, your ability to communicate fully, strike up conversations with strangers, breakthrough your fears and do things you would never otherwise think of, take powerful decisions and literally design our own life.

Sexual energy goes a long way into shaping your confidence levels and self-esteem.

Sexual energy flows into your entire being and electrifies every organ of your body, including your eyes which display the most obvious signs of high sexuality (or the lack of it), and saturates your mind to the point where you begin to naturally connect with your positive and powerful self. The results are manifold – an increased ability to manage your emotions, enhanced creativity, positive feelings, magnified sense of self and strengthen relationships with self and others.

On the flip side, a lack of sexual energy can turn around everything above and accomplish just the opposite. People with low amounts of sexual energy generally feel low in their routine, have a very little sense of confidence, communicate badly and do not have the motivation and courage to take risks in life.

The causes of lack of sexual energy can be traced back to the old stigmas, false beliefs and dogmas brought forward and marketed by various religions and societies which term sexual energy as something which is 'sinful', 'bad' and 'shameful'. This kind of thinking can form a part of your subconscious mind and can devoid of the great benefits and pleasures which you could otherwise receive. It can cause 'guilt' which is the deadliest of all emotions.

The fact is that sexual energy is nature's greatest gift and is a way to ensure that the entire human race continues to replicate and survive.

Lack of sexual energy can take away your drive to live with joy and confidence.

It can result into a judgemental attitude, useless inhibitions, over-neediness, insecurities, anger, resentments, emotional pains, painful memories, confusions, jealousies, fears of inadequacy, rejection or failure, distrust, control and conflict, self-doubt, confusion and shame.

In the state of high sexual confidence, your entire being is magnetised and the energy forms a **sexual aura** around you. You naturally begin to attract other people, especially the opposite sex, dress better and do things which are necessary to boost your self-esteem and self-confidence. This is a natural and unconscious process, and does not require effort on your part. You just want to do it and you feel automatically motivated.

You will find people drawn to you, and opposite sex getting attracted to you, when you are blistering with sexual confidence.

In a highly charged state of sexual energy, you naturally feel poised and sure of yourself. You are more focused and less distracted by negative emotions, feelings and negative environmental effects. You work towards your life's goals with zeal and enthusiasm. You feel happiness deep inside yourself, a kind which only comes when you are feeling complete and blessed.

Sexual energy can bring you closer to divinity, make you achieve impossible – seeming goals and take you to the heights of success most people only dream about.

Sexual energy is alone the greatest foundation of a true and unshakeable self-confidence. A healthy sexual energy depicts freedom from all negativity. And when you are filled with positive energy, you naturally attract more success and abundance in your life.

Everything that you do in a state of high sexual energy will have a better feel and impact as compared to what you do in a state of low sexual energy.

The message here is clear. If you want to achieve unshakeable and unlimited amounts of self-confidence, you have to understand the mechanism of sexual energy and learn to channel it for maximum benefit.

The Masculine & the Feminine

If you just look around, you'll find men and women who are devoid of the love and attention they could get from the opposite sex. This factor alone has the power to undermine all self-confidence and belief in oneself and is literally destroying their lives.

Either these people are unable to attract the opposite sex or are attracting partners who continuously betray or add to their pains in other ways.

What's the reason behind all this and what is the solution?

The reason for this is simple. We are consistently attracting partners who are in tune with our own levels of sexual energy – which is further divided into two kinds – ***masculine*** *and* ***feminine.***

Your sexual confidence is instantly perceived by the opposite sex in unconscious ways, especially by those who are more intuitive and enlightened, by virtue of their own levels of masculine or feminine energy.

Women, especially those who have healthy amounts of feminine essence, can easily notice hidden negative personality traits of a man such as neediness, resentment, insecurity, self-doubt and low self-esteem. These traits will put off such women as the man with such a personality will naturally expect her to lead most of the time and is afraid of taking risks. Such men simply repel quality women as their lack of trust in their own masculinity and sexuality is easily picked up by women.

Such women want to feel safe in the presence of a strong masculine energy and actually want to be lead and swept away by a man who has a sense of direction and passion in life. Unfortunately, most men have lost touch with their own masculinity and are living with wrong sexual beliefs and are devoid of attracting quality women with healthy feminine essence.

Men who have an abundance of masculine energy do not tolerate lead by their partners and refuse to be controlled or manipulated. They are put off by women who are manipulative, selfish or needy, as well as those who are emotionally unstable and negative.

A man's direction in life is driven to great heights by a woman who values it, and such men are always looking for a partner who values their own sense of mission in life. If a woman acts clingy or needy and distracts them from their passion and direction of life, they are turned off.

Alternatively, men with high amounts of feminine energy naturally attract women with high masculine energy and vice–versa.

What kind of partners are you attracting in your life? By estimating your own levels and nature of energy, you can now determine this easily.

And if you are not attracting the opposite sex at all, it's not your looks, money or other materialistic things which are causing this. It is your obstructed sexual energy which is repelling the opposite sex.

These obstructions are a result of wrong sexual beliefs you may have picked up from various sources, such as conditioning into feeling guilt about your sexual desires in your childhood, a particular situation where you were humiliated for your natural interest and desire towards a member of opposite sex. It may also be just a negative programming about opposite sex which is causing this trouble.

And now, let's talk about the sources which deplete your sexual energy and how you can avoid them.

Sources That Destroy Your Sexual Energy

1. Pornography

This one comes at the head of the list simply because it's one of the most dangerous habits/addictions on this planet.

Porn is a staggering $25 billion industry, magnifying the fact that more and more men and women (yes, women) are getting addicted to porn. And this number is continuously increasing.

FACT: Many men will prefer to see porn than actually go out, meet women or have intimacy with a real, alive and breathing woman. This fact alone is mind-blowing.

Watching porn is no good than having drugs or liquor to keep oneself temporarily away from problems. The real problems still exist and continue to become gigantic.

The mind runs towards pleasure and away from pain even when the pleasure is harmful in the long term. It is up to you to make a conscious choice to see what will serve you in the long term.

If you are addicted to pornography, you are literally killing your dreams, undermining your own self-confidence, conditioning yourself into failure and scaring away many good things in life.

Watching excess porn can have a direct and instant negative effect on one's self-confidence and self-esteem.

Generally, sexually explicit material is viewed in private and with intense concentration. The person who indulges into this act gets literally 'hypnotised' because of intense focus and concentration involved. What you focus upon expands.

When somebody indulges into pornography, all his/her senses get completely involved due to the arousing nature of the material. The imagination begins to run wildly registering everything which is being viewed. Here, you may acknowledge the fact that our brains cannot distinguish between a real-world experience and a vividly imagined experience.

Repeated exposure to sexually explicit material, especially the visual form of it causes a dramatic reduction in sensitivity. This process is known as 'desensitisation' and is used internationally in psychiatric departments to help cure phobias and anxiety disorders. Once desensitisation takes place, the material with even more intensity can be tolerated. Even the person who has mental constraints about intense acts like rape becomes accustomed to it and actually begins to enjoy it.

In combination to that, the mental load that the brain has to take in creating those fantasies in combination with the tenuous physical involvement is actually a form of torture for one's mind and body simultaneously.

Men who indulge into pornography develop strong and ultra-negative beliefs about women. They unconsciously begin to see women as a sport, a toy or simply as less than human. Advertisers who show a newly launched car with a hot woman draped all over it are reinforcing the same message, "Buy one, and get both". Pornography is full of visual material which degrades women into nothings. Things like this not only degrade women but also reinforce the belief that women should be degraded.

The attractiveness of women is being valued incredibly in today's advertising and porn industry in order to make hard cash. The effect of this on minds of men who see it is powerfully simple and straight – A woman's value depends on her beauty.

As a result of all these factors combined, there is no wonder more and more men are deprived of having healthy relationships with women. Deprivation of success in this area of life dramatically reduces self-confidence and self-esteem.

The case is no different for women, even if not that intense. The results are the same – destruction of all self-confidence.

A disability to maintain a healthy attitude towards sex can completely pollute one's mental, emotional and physical health.

Just like any other bad addiction, porn provides immediate and temporary satisfaction. This habit of instant gratification is prevalent in mankind by default. It is responsible for destroying one's dreams, demolish personality and wiping out self-confidence.

The problem is that this EASY way of seeking pleasure becomes a habit so quickly that unconscious mind begins to avoid real world encounters and starts fearing the troubles and challenges that arise when one is actually indulging into the act of sexual communication and hence attracting a mate.

One can have a wonderful time watching porn while the brain goes through a typical fall towards destruction. The habit of watching porn has destroyed many marriages and relationships. Pornography is not meant for enjoying sex but to enjoy more and more pornography. I personally like to call it a dream killer.

Freedom from porn addiction can only happen when one begins to become aware of the fact that it's only an empty replacement for true love. It's a sign of immaturity and causes inhibition in natural mental development of human brain.

In order to succeed with the opposite sex, as far as one's love and sex life is concerned, one must neglect pornography completely and any mental or physical acts that accompany it. The results are amazing, dramatic and extremely rewarding and manifest simultaneously in all other areas of one's life.

Those who have come out of this addiction by force of their will power and re-directing their focus into more important and enticing things of life, such as one's goals or by going through a systematic learning to get comfortable and successful with the opposite sex have reported extremely powerful and positive effects.

An increased desire to live fully, to appreciate nature and the presence of other human beings, ability to live in the **now** – in this very moment and a sudden increase in one's awareness and mental ability are some of those rewards that come as a result of this freedom.

2. Negative thoughts

If you have been into depression, you know what I am talking about here.

Depressions cause a blockage in the necessary hormones which channel your sexual energy. Negative thoughts cause small and big states of depression at continuous levels and assassinate your sexual energy.

Depression is actually nothing but a result of what you focus upon in any moment and how you use your physiology. The human body was never meant to tolerate the intensely wrong posture the body maintains when in depression in combination with a lack of proper breathing. It's a habit which the mind and body have been conditioned into. In short, depression is just a bad habit which can be turned around easily.

If you stand or sit straight with your head held high and with a big smile at your face, it will become impossible to feel negative or depressed. If you maintain this posture continuously, you will never feel depressed again.

If you can't smile all the time (well, nobody can), do this. Think **only** positive thoughts and maintain the right body posture. Breathe deeply and evenly.

Whenever you encounter a negative thought, mentally command yourself by saying something like **"Cancel"** and then think a thought opposite to that. This is called **'opposite thinking'** and has the power to powerfully affect your entire life.

In addition to that, do this simple exercise regularly for some amazing results. Stand in the front of the mirror and put a big smile on your face. Do it even if you have to force it for five minutes twice daily.

3. Taking too many medicines/prescriptions

If you are getting into this, you probably have no idea what kind of effect these little tablets are putting on your sexual energy. Even heavy smoking, excess liquor or drugs can kill off your libido once and forever. So do some medicines when taken in excess.

Getting out of these addictions is beyond the scope of this book. If you or someone you know and care about is facing this challenge, I recommend you immediately seek professional help.

4. Bad experiences in short-term or long-term relationships

Someone who has been through one or more bad experiences in relationships begins to associate negative things with sex and intimacy which are the foundations of all sexual energy. This causes a great disruption in the flow of sexual energy and causes a serious lack thereby affecting all parts of personality, causing things like depression, helplessness, problematic personality and a reduced desire to live.

If you have been there or have seen a friend go through the above situation(s), you understand where I am coming from here. Once again, it's time to go deep in the realm of your own mind and deciding to take control of this area of your life, once and forever!

I have personally experienced and seen many others having their entire lives altered by failure in relationships. It's like an everyday story where each and every person who goes through it feels he / she feels like nothing worst could happen to anyone than this, in spite of the fact that everyday thousands of men and women go through this.

Usually this results in a negative conditioning of mind and creates blocks in the path of any positive development in one's every other relationship in life.

I recommend that you immediately set a goal to get out of this, write down your intention (really, write it down) and begin to consciously take control of your thoughts and feelings. Refuse to live with this.

5. Negative conditioning

The greatest obstacle in the path of developing a sexual confidence is your own negative conditioning about sex. This can include negative beliefs about sex as well as negative emotions like guilt or shame about sexual things.

As talked above, negative beliefs about opposite sex and sex in general can cause serious inhibitions in one's life. Guilt or Shame – the two deadly emotions are generally reinforced by various sources in one's childhood and continue to haunt the person for the rest of his life.

May be you feel uncomfortable, nervous and stuck in presence of the opposite sex? If yes, have you ever wondered why?

Do you feel that you do not have the ability to attract the person you admire? Does fear of rejection haunts you? Does a fear of unknown appears from nowhere whenever you are about to approach that someone from the opposite sex?

If you answered 'Yes' to any of the above questions, you suffer from what we call a 'social block' when it comes to sex, sexual confidence and sexual energy.

What's the way out of it?

Knowledge

In the light of knowledge, all your negative beliefs about sex and sexuality will wash away.

What kind of negative beliefs?

Here's an example,

If you are a man, do you have this nasty belief that women don't like sex?

If you are a woman, have you been trained into believing that all men are the same? (and want only one thing).

These are just random but true, wildly spread examples. These negative beliefs about the opposite sex are doing nothing but destroying your own sexual life. Write down all these beliefs and begin to change them one by one (read the chapter on 'beliefs'). You will soon step into the light of knowledge, awakened.

If you want to be irresistible to opposite sex, work on your beliefs first. The fear of rejection also stems from some inner beliefs. Beside the AS IF pattern, know that if somebody rejects you, it's just a personal opinion and has nothing to do with you.

Nobody can know about you really in a matter of seconds, or in days for instant. Keep assuming that you are irresistible to the opposite sex and your actions will begin to follow.

If you are still wondering, then pay careful attention to how your negative thoughts manifest themselves around the opposite sex and drive it away. Here you are just changing your thought patterns and everything else changes by itself. This is the law of attraction in action and it's more scientific and true than anyone might believe it is. Use it to your advantage, not against you.

If you really want to understand the concepts of attraction and how to use them in your life, whether you are a man or woman, I highly suggest that you check out the resources section.

Again, if you are serious about this area of your life, I highly recommend that you go for specific education in this area.

The Secret of Personal Magnetism

Have you ever wondered how some people radiate an appealing energy that seems to attract everyone around? It's the powerful energy of sheer magnetism flowing out of their beings.

All magnetism is a result of abundance of properly channelled sexual energy, being allowed to flow freely through the entire being. A magnetic personality is a combination of confidence and healthy amounts of sexual energy.

When you are free of all your insecurities, you naturally begin to emit an aura of self-confidence. This confidence when mixed with sexual energy forms an **aura** around you and you naturally begin to attract and draw the opposite sex and people in general towards you. You literally become a human magnet.

SEX APPEAL is nothing but a result of healthy amounts of sexual confidence. So is **MAGNETISM,** a result of fine mixture of sexual confidence and sexual energy.

Visualise Yourself As 'Attractive'

Your subconscious mind is waiting to be commanded into action. If you just go ahead and begin to see yourself as ' ATTRACTIVE', very soon your mind will begin to believe it and make it happen for you. You will naturally begin to attract resources and circumstances which increase your sexual confidence and you will begin to become magnetic. This is the law of attraction at its best.

The following exercise has the power to change you in a matter of three weeks. Use it and email me with the results you get.

Close your eyes for the next 5 minutes and see yourself as a magnet. Actually see yourself walking around in a social setting and seeing the opposite sex becoming aware of you. As you walk inside, your entire being which is radiating an unstoppable magnetic energy, engulfing everyone around, is making the opposite sex mad out of attraction.

You naturally attract the opposite sex.

You are irresistible.

You are magnetic.

Continue to see yourself as powerful and magnetic and as you go through your everyday life, your energy keeps on increasing and becoming more powerful.

Fill in more and more and more details into the exercise and make it more and more real for your mind. Your mind cannot distinguish between a real life experience and a vividly imagined scenario.

So just go ahead and trick your mind. If 'tricking' sounds bad to you, consider 'helping' it out getting what it wants. Whatever you feel right – just do it. Do it everyday before you go to sleep and after you wake up for 21 days straight and notice the difference.

And now, if you have ever wondered what makes a confident human being brim with an everlasting energy that separates him from the crowd of the world, it's time to discover…

9

THE SECRET OF A NEVER-ENDING ENERGY

"When you allow yourself to begin to dream big dreams, creatively abandon the activities that are taking up too much of your time, and focus your inward energies on alleviating your main constraints, you start to feel an incredible sense of power and confidence."

—Brian Tracy

Imagine a basketball player running haphazardly in the playing court with no basket around. That's the life of a man with no goal. Life may be compared to the basketball court, and as long as you are there, you got to have a basket otherwise all that you will find is struggle, confusion and puzzlement.

In today's world, life is a constant series of ups and downs. Everywhere there is chaos, people running around and everyone seems to be in more hurry than the fastest train in the world.

Can you believe that only a handful of them actually know where they are going?

More than 95% of the world's total population moves around without having any sense of direction in life. This is a matter of great concern and amazement but since it is so common, it's taken as a normal thing.

What Do You Want?

Life is consistently asking you this question. Everything you possess, your conditions and circumstances are the answers you have chosen to give to this question. You have exactly in your possession what you have always asked from life, nothing less, nothing more.

Ask a student who's good in academics, his goals in life and whether he or she wants to become a doctor or an engineer. How many of them realise what they actually want to do in their lives? Are their goals actually their own? Are they living what they think will bring them most financial rewards, respect and satisfaction in life?

What do you want to be in your life? Or is what you are doing resonates with the inner YOU? If given the opportunity to change and do anything you want, will you change it this moment?

A large portion of the world is doing things that it doesn't want. Either the problem is finances or it is a sense of no direction in life. These people literally drag themselves through their entire lives, never realising that life could be more compelling, full of wonders and beautiful challenges that could fill them with energy and power, if only they decided to make it so.

Job satisfaction is the word you can hear often from people who work in the corporate world. But often this satisfaction is counted in terms of the paycheck they receive at the end of the month and the work they have to do in order to get it.

I have only met a few people who actually love and enjoy their jobs or business and are putting their full potential into it, and to no amazement or surprise, these are the people who know the secret you are about to learn in this chapter. These people not only enjoy their work, but they draw from it a deep sense of fulfillment, happiness and positive energy.

However, most people spend their lives running after goals which disappoint them as soon as they have reached them. They suddenly realise that this is not what they had wanted. What they actually want, to their heart's desire is somewhere else. And most of the times, it's either too late to determine what they want, let alone embark upon a journey to get it.

What is the missing element in these people's lives?

What is that source which if uncovered shall fill them with unlimited confidence, a sense of true direction and a never-ending energy?

Are you willing to learn it?

The secret is a deep sense of being connected to your ultimate purpose in life.

True self-confidence is hardly true before it is connected to one's ultimate purpose in life which serves as an outlet for it to come out and make things happen.

Your purpose in life is the reason you are here on this earth. Mother Teresa knew her purpose in life and true enough, she accomplished it to her very last breath. Mahatma Gandhi revealed his purpose when he was thrown out of the train he had bought a first-class ticket for, and he did it by freeing his country.

There are countless examples of people throughout history who have made a difference in the world through their mysterious capability of making impossible things happen. They are the people who possessed an unshakeable self-confidence which made them accomplish everything they decided upon.

And the secret of their accomplishments, their energy and their inner strength was their ability to connect and draw motivation from their purpose in life.

Life's Purpose – the Reason of Your Existence

Do you wonder what revealing your purpose can do for you in your life? Upon realising your purpose in life, you will begin to magnetically and automatically draw the universal energies and locked up inner potential which has been hiding inside you for years.

Unless you uncover your purpose, you will never feel a sense of fulfilment. Something will always seem to be missing, no matter what you do and accomplish.

Driven by your purpose you will feel an unending joy that comes from knowing the reason you are here on this earth for. And with it will come a sense of fulfilment, success and a never-ending energy which will keep you automatically motivated without any effort on your part.

You will always be full of energy and confidence. You will be a source of inspiration to others. You will draw everything that you want in your life like a magnet, easily and comfortably. Each and every day of your life will be a success and add to your life in various ways.

Have you heard of Midas, the king? He had the power to touch anything and turn it into gold. Amazingly, this is what happens when you are connected to your purpose in life. Everything you will ever want will be drawn to you. In short, you will begin to get 'lucky', as others will think you are.

How to Uncover Your Life's Purpose

In this chapter, you are going to uncover the ultimate purpose of your life. In addition, you shall receive instructions on how to set compelling goals for yourself which help you fulfil your purpose and create a sense of direction in life.

Firstly, realise this: Your subconscious mind already knows your purpose. If you have ever seen a small child playing with his/her toys, you can easily figure out what the subconscious mind of that child is trying to reveal. This is a natural urge of that inner purpose residing in every one of us, which seeks ways out through natural interests.

In childhood, when the conscious mind is still learning, natural subconscious desires express themselves through many ways without resistance. Have you ever noticed how curious you were as a child? What was your greatest curiosity? What was it that you always wanted to make happen? What were your longings, inner desires and natural interest?

As we move through life, bombarded with false limitations put on us by the dominating elements in our life such as our parents or the society, we tend to get disconnected from our purpose of life. This purpose is still there though, lying under the layers of these beliefs and limitations.

In order to uncover your purpose, you need to dive deeper into your subconscious mind. Your purpose may not be revealed to you consciously right away as it is usually hidden deeper. But it will reveal itself for sure, so stay motivated.

As I am writing these words, I am thinking about my own childhood and the curiosities I had then. After I was able to reveal my inner purpose of life, I was literally amazed and astonished by the way it connected to my interests, curiosities and behaviours when I was a child. It has never failed to amaze me whenever I think about it.

Your inner purpose can be revealed to you consciously in various ways. One of them is your own conscious effort to find it, as you will do it in this chapter. Another way is a deep setback in life, which is usually a result of a turnaround in circumstances (and a result of your own dominating thoughts) in which suddenly your inner purpose and potential is revealed to you. However, this isn't in your direct control.

Mahatma Gandhi was thrown out of the train by the British when he realised that his whole sole purpose of life was to free his country.

I recommend though, that you set yourself up consciously to discover your purpose in life, if it hasn't been revealed to you yet. It's worth the effort and the rewards are too great to list here.

Finding Your Purpose

The first step is to take an inventory of your natural hobbies, interests and longings in your life. Take your journal and your pen/pencil and list them now.

Do you find something in which you can get so engrossed that you tend to lose track of the time? What interests you deeply?

What is it that doing it gives you an inner excitement, enthusiasm and joy? This could be a clue to your purpose in life, or the purpose itself.

Look back to your childhood. Think about your natural curiosities and interests. What did you want to become in your life then when there were no limitations?

Now answer this question:

"If you had only 6 months to live, had adequate finances to live by comfortably through this time and were given the choice to do ONE thing that will make you feel you have made a difference, what would you choose to do?"

This question is very powerful. Actually, most of the people I have asked this question from tend to get unstable and confused and most of the times, I get no answers.

In fact, in my experience, out of hundreds of people that I have asked this from, only two or three of them were able to clearly state their choice and seemed totally comfortable with it.

It's OK if you cannot answer this now. All the above process is to let your unconscious know what you are up to. Your unconscious has learned to ignore your conscious input and needs to be stimulated before it can begin to listen to you again. This is a process of stimulating your unconscious mind and preparing it to reveal your purpose to you. It is a totally normal process and you don't need to worry about any of the previous or following steps, at least not more than you worry about screaming in terror when you see a horror movie.

Read the above lines again before you move ahead.

Now do this: Keep on asking this question to yourself now onwards until you receive an answer which fills you with an inner feeling of enthusiasm, joy and excitement. Here's a tool which can help you get to it faster.

"Move forward in time...and imagine yourself lying on your deathbed. See yourself surrounded with your loved ones and your relatives.

These are your last moments, your last breaths. You know you are going to part with your body within a few minutes.

Take a moment and immerse yourself into this feeling.

And now, you close your eyes and look back at your life, trying to determine how your life has been, whether it has been worthwhile or not. You want to see whether you have made a difference in the world with your presence? Have you lived fully?

Now answer this, **"What is it that you would like to see when you look back to your life?**

Drift back 10 years in time and see what would you like to see yourself doing? The thing that makes you feel fulfilled and connected to an inner source of never-ending energy.

Keep moving back until you are at this point in your life, while you are listening (or reading) to these words. What do you want to see?

Spend a few moments here. Take your time. Be fully immersed in the process.

And now as you listen to these words, ask your unconscious to reveal your purpose in life.

As you count from 1 to 5, let the energy come back into your body and your mind, and whenever you feel comfortable, you can open your eyes."

I recommend that you do the above visualisation until you have actually received your answer. Your unconscious will reveal your answer right when you are in the middle of your visualisation, or when you ask from it at the end of the session, or while you are done with the exercise and are going through your day-to-day life. Usually this will come as an 'aha' moment, a deep inspiration or a hunch accompanied by the feelings of joy, enthusiasm and fulfilment.

All you have to do is to stay focused for any signals from your unconscious mind. In addition to this, copy and print out the following message:

"I am slowly becoming aware of my true purpose in life. While I go through my normal life, I will become aware of the clues I receive from my mind. I will have dreams which will make me even more aware of my life's purpose. I will develop a strong, conscious feeling of my purpose. As my purpose is revealed to me consciously, I will begin to feel compelled towards new directions, pathways and opportunities. I will keep an open mind and accept these guidelines and walk through them with confidence. As I become aware of my purpose, my entire being will radiate more joy, happiness and enthusiasm."

Read the above message 10-20 times before you go to sleep and after you wake up in the morning. Do it not less than 10 times and there's no need to do it more than 20 times.

Alternatively, watch out your member's area for a guided visualisation, the username and password to which you received in your email when you bought this book. We're not done yet.

In order to take a complete conscious control of your life, you must begin now by defining what exactly you want from your life.

What Do You Really Want?

"Obstacles are those frightful things you see when you take your eyes off your goal."

—Henry Ford

Everybody has dreams but only a few achieve them. Is it a matter of luck? Hardly.

Here's an opportunity to uncover your hidden dreams and bring them into the light of awareness where you can create specific plans to achieve them – one by one.

Following your dreams require an intelligent mixture of clarity and preciseness about your goal, a supporting belief system and a motivated, persistent effort. Setting goals put you directly behind the steering wheel of your own life and give you a conscious control of everything. In this section, we'll be defining your goals in life.

Remember, true confidence never exists in an aimless, vaguely defined life. Once you set your goals and begin to achieve them one by one, your confidence will continue to soar.

In order to produce a sense of true and unshakeable confidence in yourself, you must take a conscious control of your life. Setting and accomplishing new goals will accomplish just that for you.

Goals unlock your inner potential and create an unbelievable momentum in your life. They are the directions towards which your mind strides by bringing out your inner potential.

Different people look at life in entirely different ways. While some people let things happen to them, others go out and make things happen. It's very important to have an understanding of which group you belong to.

Goals put you into total control of your own life. And when you feel you are in control of your life and events, you will feel a natural confidence surging inside you enabling you to achieve even more next time.

Ask yourself the following question:

What do you really want to get out of life?

A clear vision and a well-defined mission will help you realise the real purpose of your life. Both your vision and mission should express your purpose for existence.

Following is a series of questions for you to ask yourself in order to do some soul searching and to give yourself some insights into what you are all about and why you are here:

- "When I grow up, I want to be a pilot." As a child, what did you dream of becoming?
- Which three people do you think have influenced your life the most and why?
- If you could choose your career and get paid whatever you wanted, what would you opt for?
- What are your top three achievements in life so far? What was so special about them?
- Doing what makes you the happiest in life?
- Who are the three people who you admire the most? What are their characteristics and qualities you admire so much?
- Have you ever helped someone less fortunate than you? If yes, what did you do? If no, why not?
- List out your greatest strengths?
- What steps should you take in life to maximise your strengths?
- What is that one thing for which you would be willing to put everything on the block for? Why?
- Imagine that all the time you spent till now comes back to you. How would you utilise it now? What would you do with the time this second time?
- There are sure to be results/events in your life you are happy about? What are these? Which are the results/events you are unhappy about?
- Is there a word of advice you have picked up from your life so far that you want to pass on to the world?
- Name one thing you value the most in life?
- What would you really like to do with your life?

Answering the questions given above will give you a clear idea about yourself.

The whole point of getting you to think about those questions was to really get you to think about what you want and wanted from your life.

10

THE ART OF CONFIDENT LIVING

The Power Principles

You are now going to learn some really powerful principles using which you can literally become the master of your life.

These principles come from various sources – and have been carefully extracted to compel one create a personality that naturally exudes power.

These principles are power attitudes – ***they are a way of living.*** Adopt them and make them a part of your life. Each one of them has the ability to empower your entire being

Here's for the life of your dreams...

1. Live in the Eternal Now

"If you are still talking about what you did yesterday,
you haven't done much today."

—Anonymous

Have you ever seen a child playing? Children seem to have no worries about anything at all. Everything in their life is just perfect and they are enjoying every moment of it.

Don't you wish that you could squeeze out infinite joy and happiness from each and every moment of your life?

We are all aware of this secret in our childhood but tend to forget it as we grow up. This secret is the key to all happiness and joy – and your key to confident and powerful living as well.

To live in the present, in the eternal NOW, is one of the greatest gifts you can give to yourself.

"Let us not look back in anger, nor forward in fear,
but around in awareness."

—James Thurber

You are not your mind, nor your body

Just like your hands and legs, or any other body part for instance, your mind is simply a tool which helps you in living through this life. You are however, **not** your body or mind but detached from both.

So what in the world are you?

I was introduced to this amazing and life-changing secret in the book *The Power of Now* by Eckhart Tolle. Many other books have been written on this subject and I consider myself fortunate to have learned this great principle.

Normally, majority of the population of this world makes an ultimate mistake by identifying oneself with one's body and mind. When you say, "I am [your name]", you are not referring to yourself but the body you live in.

Similarly, you are not your mind. All your feelings, emotions and everything going on inside it is not **you**. In short, you are separate from both your mind and body.

By understanding this concept, you are now going to take a firm and long step towards self-mastery and to a life of total confidence.

You are an energy living through this life and using your body and mind in the process. Some refer to it as 'soul'. Give yourself any name you feel right.

When you eat, you use your body. When you think, you use your mind.

Just imagine for a moment. If you saw someone continuously slapping himself, what would you call that person? Insane? Mad?

Hand is a tool you must only use when you need it. If it goes out of control, you will definitely seek a remedy for it.

The same is with your mind. Your mind is a tool for thinking and other related functions. When it goes out of control, making you feel things you don't want to feel, taking you through emotions that hurt you or torturing you with its continuous mental chatter – you must realise that you need to control it and put an end to this silent insanity.

The solution is simple and just needs some practice.

Your mind goes out of control by consistently worrying about the future or by dwelling on the past. By forcing it to live in the realm of present, where life actually exists, you put your mental chatter to an immediate halt.

From now onwards, make it a point to be fully present. Do not have any worries or anxieties about 'tomorrow'. Your subconscious mind that holds all your inner potential doesn't have to do anything with the past or future. It can only exist, operate and create its magic in the present.

It's great to have goals for tomorrow but to live in the tomorrow is an entirely different thing – something that you must totally refrain yourself to do.

Living in the present helps your unconscious to put forth all your inner potential and help you do and create things which you would otherwise never be able to accomplish. It releases your entire being from the locks of worry and makes you lose yourself into the present task at hand.

Have you ever found yourself lost into an interesting novel, a movie or something that really held your attention? You were in the present at that particular moment. Notice how you enjoyed doing that thing.

"We crucify ourselves between two thieves:
regret for yesterday and the fear of tomorrow."

—Fulton Oursler

Pay careful attention to what is happening 'now'. Anything can happen tomorrow but your mind needs to be fully aware of what is already happening in the present moment.

Dale Carnegie started his wonderful book – *How to Stop Worrying and Start Living* with the chapter **Live in Day Tight Compartments.** It means that you should only be concerned about your 24-hour cycle of the day and not worry about what is going to happen tomorrow.

If you take this advice to never ever plan for your future again – **that's exactly NOT** what this principle is trying to tell you. You must know your goals which will happen in the future but to obtain them on time you must act in the present. You cannot act in your past or future. You can visualise your goals and see yourself acting as will like yourself in the future for few minutes a day, but most of your time must go into living in the present moment.

Practice becoming consciously aware of everything happening around you and you shall unlock the key to infinite power. Even when you are feeling tense, or find yourself unable to act the way you must in a key situation – Stop and ask, "What exactly is happening around me? Why am I here and what am I responding to?"

Listen to the sounds occurring around you, smell the odour you have not being paying attention to before and see things around you more carefully and clearly. Feel the floor beneath your feet when you stand or walk. Involve all your senses in the now and command yourself to "Stay in the now".

Check your breathing – Are you breathing fully? Watching your breath has an immediate effect on your sense of presence.

To check whether you are in the present moment or not, ask – "Am I fully present?" Presence will always follow this question and you will feel yourself drawn into the now as you ask it.

If you were looking for a magic cure to all your worries, nervousness and anxieties – this is exactly what you need. Most of the worries and anxieties exist in remaining concerned about the future and trying to accomplish things which cannot be done in the present.

Stop and think about what exactly you are responding to. **Are you responding to something in the present or something that happened in the past or something that may happen in the future?**

Living in the now is a habit that you can develop. Your mind will continue to resist at first and take your attention to past and future – it's his job, never mind. Train it to this new habit and reap the great rewards that follow.

2. Live in your Reality

The credit for this concept goes to David De Angelo, of Double Your Dating Fame.

The world is exactly what you decide to see it as.

You have already read the chapter on beliefs. So you already know that nothing in this world has any meaning except what you choose to give to it. It's your interpretation of an external circumstance, happening or a condition of your life that determines its effect on you.

Two different persons can look at the word 'fire' in two different ways. For the person who sees fire as something useful will respond differently to it than the person who has been through an experience of getting badly burned. It means different things to different people and that's what makes all the difference in the world.

Living in your reality is a concept of ultimate power. When you understand your ability to choose your beliefs consciously in order to see the world from the best possible angle – where you exist as a powerful entity, you literally act it out in the real world.

Most people in this world live in the reality of those who are superior or powerful than them or perceived as powerful by them. Your perceptions define how much power something or someone has upon you.

Your reality is your personal world where your consciously chosen beliefs lie. When you live those beliefs out through your behaviour and actions, you project a powerful image to the outer external world. In your world, you are free to do, be or have anything you want. You decide how others behave with you and react to you in order to stay in your world. If someone doesn't accept your reality, you wouldn't change it just for that single person.

How powerful your reality is depends directly upon the strength of your beliefs.

Are your beliefs powerful and useful in nature?

Are they serving you and others simultaneously?

At the same time, are they helping you live out with your fullest potential?

Have they been specifically chosen after careful consideration to reflect who you really are?

Living in your reality makes this world seem like a piece of cake for you. You live in your world and everybody else is a guest in it.

Here are a few beliefs which you can adopt right now for building up your personal reality. Add your own and follow the above checklist of questions to confirm their validity and usefulness in your life. And using the techniques in chapter 6, keep on strengthening them until they have become a part of who you are.

1. **I am the ultimate master of everything in my life.**
2. **I live with complete integrity and display inner strength at all time.**
3. **I am passionate about life and the challenges it offers. I love to master them and grow more powerful in the process.**
4. **I expect complete respect for me, my time and my belongings from everyone I deal with – my family, friends and professional relations.**
5. **I am happy, stable and at complete peace – no matter what the external circumstances of my life may be.**
6. **I make things happen rather than waiting for them to happen by themselves.**
7. **I deserve just the best of everything in this world and I always follow high standards.**
8. **I focus only on the positive in life.**
9. **I live each day and each moment to its fullest, as if it were the last I am living.**
10. **I believe in a power higher than everything in this universe and expect it to bring me everything which I ever desire from my life, in ways which are for the highest good of me and everyone else involved.**

3. Live on the Edge

Here's a beautiful poem that has made a huge difference in the way I live my life and has become an integral part of my life's journey.

This poem was originally written by a little girl who suffered from CANCER and had only 6 months to live. "She'll never make it to the prom, or graduate from high school, or get married and have a family of her own." I read when I received this poem in my email.

To live your life to the fullest is the key message of this beautiful and touching poem.

SLOW DANCE

Have you ever watched kids,
On a merry go round?
Or listened to the rain,
Slapping on the ground?
Ever followed a butterfly's erratic flight?
Or gazed at Sun into the fading night?
You better slow down,
Don't dance so fast.
Time is short,
The music won't last.
Do you run through each day,
On the fly?
When you ask: How are you?
Do you hear the reply?
When the day is done,
Do you lie in your bed?
With the next hundred chores,
running in your head?
You'd better slow down,
Don't dance so fast.
Time is short.
The music won't last.
Ever told your child,
We'll do it tomorrow?
And in your haste,
Not see his sorrow?
Ever lost touch,
Let a good friendship die?
Cause you never had time,

To call and say 'Hi'?
You'd better slow down.
Don't dance so fast.
Time is short.
The music won't last.
When you run so fast to get somewhere,
You miss half the fun of getting there.
When you worry and hurry throughout your day,
It is like an unopened gift thrown away.
Life is not a race,
Do take it slower.
Hear the music,
Before the song is over.

We really don't have enough time to waste on this earth. Life is like a burning candle which is going to end one day, no matter who you are. Your greatest purpose in life is to explore your fullest potential and in order to do that; you must remind yourself that anything that you worry about isn't going to matter when you die.

When you keep yourself from taking the risks that could help you discover your inner potential or achieve whatever you desire from life, you are depriving yourself from most of the fun and joy that life wants to offer you.

Decide to live your life today as if you were living the last day of it and you will suddenly set yourself up for maximum performance. Anything which is irrelevant or an obstacle to living your life to your fullest potential is suddenly put to a halt by your mind. You act in the present automatically and that's where all your power lies.

Also, learn to take risks when it is necessary for your goals. Life is going to end one day and you will ultimately repent for what you haven't done than what you tried upon and failed. Look at your past life.

Are there things you wanted to do but didn't for any reason? You could have done them and failed, doesn't matter – but even failure is reserved for those who try at the first place.

There is actually no failure. There's even nothing called as success. There are only **results** of the actions you take and you can always keep on adjusting them until you have achieved the results you desire.

Learn to live at the edge, starting from now.

4. Decide To Be Happy, No Matter What

Your inner happiness is a result of your awakening to the fact that you are the ultimate controller and master of your life.

Happiness is a decision only you can make. It does not depend upon any external circumstances or conditions. True happiness and joy always comes from within and there are things which you can adopt for bringing maximum happiness in your everyday life.

By understanding that anything happening outside your internal world is an illusion and deciding that nothing has the power to affect your state of mind until you specifically allow it to, you hold the key to ultimate happiness in your life.

Your inner world is completely dependent upon the choices you make. Your choices give way to the thoughts that ultimately shape your entire life. By choosing to being happy and at peace, no matter what, you throw open the gates to extreme abundance.

First of all, learn to embrace your existence on this earth. Fall in love with yourself. You are an ultimate creation of God. It doesn't matter who you are and what you are at this moment. What matters is where you want to be. And you can do that by virtue of your own thoughts. It's a power that you possess and can use whenever you want.

Quit worrying and living in any kind of fears. If something has to happen in the future, it hasn't happened yet. Don't contribute into a negative happening by using your thought power. Even when you focus upon what is wrong in the world, you are adding into it the power of your thought. Whatever you focus upon expands.

If you are worrying about something which has happened already, correct it. Anything in your past can be undone by a simple shift in your inner world of thoughts.

If you don't know how to make something happen, live in the joy and excitement where you are expecting a whole new way to open up. It will open up if you decide and feed it with your positive thoughts of expectancy.

Learn to laugh with your heart. Help others laugh and have fun. This is probably the greatest gift you can give to yourself and others. Be a person who is known for his upbeat, magnetic personality.

I have personally been and have seen many others wondering about the secret of creating a magnetic personality that naturally attracts others. One of the greatest secrets of such a personality is your genuine capability to radiate inner happiness and joy which automatically inspire the same in others in your presence.

True happiness and joy comes from the spiritual you. "You are not a human being having a spiritual experience, but a spiritual being having a human experience", said **Dr. Wayne Dyer,** in his magnificent book *You'll See It When You Believe In It*. Connect to the spiritual you where all power exists.

What you see as real is simply a manifestation of your or someone else's thoughts. Your body is also a result of this manifestation and so are the experiences your body and brain go through in life. You are more than your bodies and behaviours. You are literally impenetrable. Nothing that ever happens can withdraw you from the true happiness and joy that contains within you.

Focus on abundance and true happiness. Choose joy over worry and fears. And you have the key to ultimate power.

5. Learn to Forgive

Forgiveness is the most powerful symbol of a healthy, powerful and super-confident personality.

Living with grudges about what has happened to you in the past, for other people or even for yourself is a cause of eroding your self-confidence and filling you with rage and negative emotions.

When you forgive, you suddenly claim infinite power. The reason for this is that you send a clear signal to your mind, "I am in control." This is **very powerful**. All our lives, we are striving to achieve control. When you forgive, you take a firm step towards building a life full of choices. The moment you forgive with all your heart, you literally have taken control of your entire emotional system and have mastered the outside circumstances by deciding to forgive.

When you forgive, you accept all responsibility for everything which has happened until now. This acceptance reinforces the fact that you are always in control and everything that will happen in the future is **also** in your total control.

"You have one advantage over the person who has done wrong to you. You have the power to forgive that person."

—Napoleon Hill

If you hold any negative emotions, rage or grudge against someone, forgive them. Close your eyes and affirm your ability to change your world by the virtue of your thoughts alone. Say "I forgive [name of the person] for everything with all my heart and by the God's truth." Say this three times.

If you hold any grudge for yourself and most people do, forgive yourself. Just say, "I forgive [your name] for everything with all my heart by the God's truth." Say this three times and notice your feelings. You can use the same script for others (just insert the correct name).

6. Make Your Presence In This World Worth It

If you have read so far and have been applying the techniques mentioned regularly, you are already on your way to developing the life of your dreams.

Your presence in this world is already divine. You possess incredible gifts and abilities which you are passionately exploring inside you and bringing them together to live your life to the fullest.

We all have been at a point in our lives when we really needed a hand to guide us into the right direction and show us the way to light. I was fortunate enough to be introduced to the personal development industry when I needed such a direction in my life.

May be you have been there too and learned a way out somehow – through a personal mentor who guided you, a seminar, a book or a programme. It might just be this book or anything else which has made a positive difference in your life.

Whatever it is, you now have the capability to join the army of those who are committed to make a difference in others lives. No, you don't necessarily have to become a writer, speaker or do anything to reach people and help them. You can help others achieve their goals and dreams in life by being wherever you are right now – in any profession you are.

And nevertheless, whenever you do so, you will always receive back a higher return. This is the Law of Increasing Returns in full-blown action – and it takes care of everything without you ever have to bother about anything.

If you are a manager or someone who has people working for you – you can help them become better, organised and more efficient by sharing what you have learned to discover your inner potential.

You can apply these techniques and others that you learn in your personal development journey as the basis of your organisational structure and let your business flourish at doubled, tripled and even quadrupled rates.

Make it a habit to appreciate others whenever you have an opportunity. Appreciation is probably the greatest gift you can give to anyone. It reinforces one's sense of self-worth, raises self-esteem and boosts self-confidence – all at the same time!

You can share these principles with those you love and help them realise that they hold the key to their lives. Apply these principles in your own relationships and see it blooming.

If you find someone in trouble and believe your advice can help him or her, go ahead and use your knowledge to help that person. It is hard to express in words the pleasure you obtain by knowing that you have made a positive difference in someone's life.

Every time when somebody comes over and says, "Thank you. You have changed my life", it makes me feel a tremendous sense of inner joy and power. Think about it – it's a whole life that you have been able to influence for good.

There is a great joy in giving back what you have learned most willingly in your life. The rewards are too great to be mentioned here and you have to experience this personally in order to understand it fully.

Even if you have just started, start sharing the things you learn with those you feel could need it. Helping others achieve something is a clear signal to your subconscious that you already possess it in abundance. You can only give what you already have in plenty. The more you share it, the more you attract it in your life.

By sharing the techniques discussed in this book or other information which has had a powerful and positive impact on your life, you can add tremendous value to the world you live in. You can help others find their inner potential, work with zeal and enthusiasm, explore their inner happiness and live fully by committing to share this information with others.

The best way to do is to first apply all these things in your life and become a role model for others. When you do that, others will automatically begin to wonder what's so special about you. When they become curious, be willing to share what you have.

Bring smiles on others faces and help them live fully. Make them laugh and have fun around you. This must now be your greatest purpose and goal in life.

CONCLUSION

We've come to the end of this book. I sincerely hope that this journey has been as wonderful for you as it has been for me. I know how incredibly amazing it is to see the hidden confidence within one self manifesting in life and bringing great, previously only dreamed of things.

I believe you have been able to experience that magical difference in you while we talked, learned, laughed and sometimes argued through the words of this book.

However, your journey has actually just begun. This is not the end, but the beginning. Confidence is a never-ending journey and as your life will pass by, you will find yourself realising that you always have something more to discover inside you. There is no limit to your inner potential and this is no understatement.

From this point ahead, you are now on your own, as I had promised at the beginning.

However, ever you need any support, assistance or help in your life's journey – remember that I am only an email or phone call away. I'll always be there, as my mentors have always been and are for me. It's always a real pleasure to hear from you, really. So feel free to contact me whenever you want.

I invite you to visit my websites www.confidencewithin.com and www.success-mantra.com to stay updated.

I wish you everything that you ever dream of in your life!!!

To The Life of Your Ultimate Dreams...

Your friend,
Aery Prabhakar

Appendix A

THE ART OF VISUALISATION

Most of the exercises given in this book require you to understand and master the art of visualisation. The truth is, even if you think you are not good at imagining pictures, you are already a master. This section will remind you of your already existing ability to visualise successfully.

When you were a child, your imagination ran freely. You allowed your mind to exaggerate things and imagine wild things just out of curiosity. Even when you grew as an adult, your mind never lost its capability to imagine and exaggerate things. You may, however, have tended to get less conscious of your ability to imagine things.

What are fears or phobias anyways? All your fears and phobias are simply wild and uncontrolled imaginations which were over-exaggerated. Have you ever got your shirt stuck at a sharp corner in the dark and found yourself screaming out of fear? That's exactly what we are talking about here.

Actually, you are imagining things all day long. Think of the home you live in. Does a picture come to your mind? Can you see it clearly?

Think about your favourite car. Is the picture there? Now change its colour in your mind. Take it through five different colours – you can use red, yellow, orange, blue and black (nothing special in them – just got them off top of my head). Now enlarge the car. Make it monster size. Actually see monsters sitting in it – having fun and singing monster songs. Make the picture moving. Now reduce the car's size slowly so that it becomes a point.

How was it? Did you have fun doing this? Why don't you go ahead and do even more funnier things you think will make the picture interesting.

If you think you are bad at making pictures, you just proved yourself wrong.

Onwards

We are specifically concerned with visualisation here which is a little ahead than simply imagining pictures in your mind.

Visualisation as an art is generally misunderstood. Although visualisation is about making pictures, it is **also** about thinking with respect to all other elements, involving all your senses in the process.

Imagination is about making pictures. But visualisation is about using all your senses, be it your ability to create mental pictures, hear sounds, feel, smell and taste. All your senses must be involved in a successful visualisation.

Bring the above picture of your car back in the eye of your mind. Now see yourself standing beside it wearing a black suit with a white shirt (like men in black). Now step inside the car and turn on the ignition. **Hear** the sound of the car getting started. Now press the accelerator and listen to the sound. Do this a few times.

One more important thing to consider is association and disassociation. A disassociated experience is when you see yourself in an experience from a third-person's point of view. That means you see yourself acting in an experience while you are standing and observing from outside. Is this what you did when you imagined the above experience of sitting and starting your car? Great.

An associated experience is a little more objective and more powerful. In this, you don't see yourself from a third person's point of view but you are there yourself experiencing the things, feeling everything in detail. An associated experience is very powerful and requires you to spend more concentration. Think about a rollercoaster ride. What do you see, hear and feel when you are sitting in a rollercoaster yourself? That's an associated experience.

Try the above exercise again. This time wear a black suit yourself and start walking towards your car. Pay attention to the stuff of the suit you are wearing. Touch and feel its texture. Feel yourself taking steps towards your car.

Now open the door and sit into it. Experience the 'new car' smell coming from the interiors of the car. Feel your back on the seat of the car. Now take the key out of your pocket, insert it and turn on the ignition. Hear the sound of your car. Press the accelerator and listen to the increasing intensity of sound.

Come back. Congratulations – you just let your mind successfully go through an actual visualisation.

Have you already noticed the difference between an associated and disassociated experience? For greatest effects, and sometimes for any effects at all, you will be using associated visualisation.

FACT: Your brain cannot distinguish between a real world experience and a deep visualisation. For it, visualisation is as good as a real world experience.

Visualisation is used by successful sports persons who continuously visualise performing each and every step of their game successfully. They imagine a successful outcome again and again in the eye of their mind, involving themselves completely into it and living it to the fullest. On the day of their performance, their mind has already done it so many times that they are able to go ahead and give their best performance with ease.

Visualisation is used by hypno-therapists for treating their patients and changing the way they experience their inner world. NLP practitioners use this to master fears and phobias, learn new skills and model their way to success in life.

Many of the exercises in this book come from hypnotherapy and NLP and each of it is very powerful when done using associated visualisation.

At first, you might struggle a little bit in getting your pictures right and even a little stressful (it's not necessary though). With practice and experience, your ability to visualise will sharpen and become more powerful.

Visualisation vs Fantasising

It is extremely important for you to understand the distinction between **visualisation** and **fantasising.**

Visualisation is a consciously controlled process of imagining key behaviours and situations as you would like them to be, followed by a concrete action plan. Visualisation involves all your senses and makes use of the fact that human mind cannot distinguish between a real world experience and a vividly imagined experience to create desired results in life.

Fantasising is something you wish you could do but know somewhere inside that you cannot. Basically, it is something you play again and again in your mind and then do **not** follow with a concrete action to make it a reality.

Delving into fantasies is mind's way of escaping from the challenges of real world and to **satisfy itself temporarily by imagining a scenario as if it is really happening.**

Let me make things a little clearer here. Fantasising gives a false sense of satisfaction. When mind is satisfied already, why would it bother to produce any real results? This is especially true when it is easier to get satisfied using imagination than face real world challenges.

The worst thing is fantasising can easily become a habit – a dangerous habit.

Visualise, not fantasise. Fantasising is the main cause of the all so called 'love' disorders and imbalances in many people's life. Sexual attraction combined with a need of love and approval, which happen to be personality disorders, is mostly misunderstood as 'love'. It can become over-hyped by one's consistent fantasising of the pleasures one gets by actually being with the person involved.

The problem occurs when these fantasies are not played in the real world due to fears and inaction. The brain goes into a strange state and gets confused and is unable to understand what's going on.

See if what is going on in your mind would be followed with concrete action or not. If not, stop it at once.

Fantasising can become a lifetime habit and kill focus and concentration, which are necessary for obtaining success in any area of your life.

Here's a question you can ask yourself to snap out of your fantasising habit. Whenever you catch yourself fantasising, stop and ask yourself– **"What is this thought trying to accomplish?"**

If you see it as a mental effort to prove yourself to others, obtain validation, fill a physical or mental need that you must actually go out and fill in the real world – **stop it at once.**

Visualise, not fantasise.

And now, it's practice time.

Practicing Visualisation

And now for practice, perform the following visualisation regularly for the next seven days.

1. Choose an everyday article/object from your home or office. Find an empty table and sit beside it with only your chosen object on it.
2. Look at it very carefully and absorb each and every detail of that object. Observe its size, shape, colour and even the shadow it puts on the table. Memorise as much of this detail as possible.
3. Now close your eyes and picture the object in the eye of your mind. Try to remember as many details as you can.
4. Still sitting with your eyes closed - take a moment to think about how you are feeling. Do you feel under any stress as you try this exercise? Do you find the exercise to be interesting?
5. OK, clear that picture from your mind and, while you are still at the table with your eyes closed, think about another everyday object in your home and, once again, try to picture it in your mind's eye in as much detail as you can.
6. When you are happy that you have a clear picture of the object, open your eyes and go and find it. How close was the picture that you painted in your mind's eye to the actual object? Also, try to identify the details which you missed in your visualisation.
7. Once again take a minute to consider how you are feeling and whether or not you find this exercise stressful.

8. Now, return to the table and once more sitting with your eyes closed try to remember and picture an object from your childhood days. Think carefully about how much of the object can you recall and whether or not you can remember the details clearly. Once you have the object in your mind's eye, see if you can place it in its original surroundings.
9. There will almost certainly be bits missing from your picture and your mind will try to fill in any gaps from your imagination. Can you tell which parts of the picture are real and are coming from your memory and which are being created by your imagination?
10. Next, picture a common everyday object, such as a vase, but this time picture an object that you have never seen before. In other words, create this object in detail in your imagination giving it size, shape and colour. Once you have the picture, imagine yourself holding the object and think about how it feels. Is it, for example, rough and heavy or smooth and light? And, once again, as you hold the object in your hands, think about how you are feeling.

Appendix B

RECOMMENDED RESOURCES

The Law of Success – Napoleon Hill
Psycho-Cybernetics – Maxwell Maltz
Double Your Dating -- David De Angelo

TEST YOUR CONFIDENCE

THE CONFIDENCE EVALUATOR

The Confidence Evaluator is an assessment to evaluate your current levels of confidence and self-esteem.

Take the test, see what your scores are and then map out a plan of action to increase your scores over the next 3 months.

Rank your current levels of confidence in each area of your life. If a sentence stands true for you, give yourself 1 point.

After you have finished reading the book and have applied the techniques discussed for at least 21 days straight, remember to come back and re-evaluate yourself again to see where you have reached.

Again, re-evaluate yourself after 3 months (or 90 days). It's optional – but you are requested to write to me the difference this book has been able to make in your self-confidence.

Self-Worth

- I love my life and I am very happy
- I am a worthwhile person
- I love being me
- I don't feel like a failure
- I am as good as other people if not better
- I can laugh at myself
- I am a positive person
- I don't worry what others think of me

- I look in the mirror and like what I see
- I am good company to be around

Self-worth score out of 10 __

Go For It!

- I am not afraid of failure
- I don't beat myself up if I make mistakes
- I don't doubt my own ability
- I know what I want in life and am moving towards it
- I am in control of my life
- I know my strengths and weaknesses
- If things don't go my way I never give up
- I've succeeded in the past and I will succeed tomorrow
- My philosophy is "You only live once"
- I am always thinking of ways to be more successful

Go for it! score out of 10 __

Communicating with Others

- I am a confident communicator
- I don't mind speaking in front of groups
- I am not afraid to say "NO" to others
- I don't get nervous when meeting strangers
- I can keep a conversation going
- I am not afraid to complain if I get bad services
- I am not frightened to speak up at meetings
- I have no problem asking for what I want on the telephone
- I have good interpersonal skills
- I am interested in what others have to say

Communicating with others score out of 10 __

Having Pleasure and Fun!

- I don't get nervous when I tell a joke
- I enjoy having fun and relaxing
- I take pleasure in my achievements
- I never think that when I experience pleasure it is undeserved
- I don't have to work hard at having fun
- When I succeed I never respond by feeling defensive or anxious
- If others don't like me having fun, that's tough!
- I make people laugh
- I regularly have fun
- I smile a lot

Having pleasure and fun score out of 10 __

Confidence at Work

- I am in control of my career
- I don't doubt my ability to do a/the job
- I don't have a problem with talking to people higher up the organisation than me
- I don't have difficulty in saying "No"
- If I lost my job today I am confident that I would get one very soon
- I don't mind speaking in front of others
- I like to do presentations
- I should be in a much higher position at work
- I know my weaknesses and I have got a plan in place to improve them
- Criticism rarely fazes me

Confidence at work score out of 10 __

Looking After Yourself

- I take in exercise at least 3 times a week
- I lead a healthy lifestyle in terms of the food I eat and I do not abuse my body with excess alcohol

- I am happy with my appearance
- I regularly visit the dentist, optician and my doctors for check-ups
- I manage my stress levels by relaxing each and every day
- I have at least 3 holidays/breaks per year
- There are no outstanding issues or problems that have not been resolved or working towards being resolved
- I do not chase my tail in terms of not having enough time
- I regularly treat myself each week to something I enjoy – clothes, CDs, massage, nails, hair, skin, etc
- I regularly assess how I am looking after myself and put a plan in place to improve

Looking after yourself score out of 10 –

Growth & Development

- I am constantly learning and growing
- I try out new things and activities all the time
- I make plans to improve myself constantly
- I know what my goals are and I am eagerly and effectively making them a reality
- I enjoy variety
- I develop the people around me so that they are more successful in their lives
- I have all the tools, aids, contacts and resources to make me a success
- I have a mentor who continually pushes me to achieve more
- I make events happen rather than wait for them to happen to me
- I regularly attend seminars, training courses and conferences to improve

Growth & Development score out of 10 __

Unfinished Business

- I am in control of my own life and my own destiny
- I could die right this moment with no regrets
- I am doing what I want, when I want
- I am really optimistic about the future
- There is nothing I am dreading or avoiding at this moment in time
- I have a plan in place to succeed in all that I do
- I am implementing my plan
- I have the energy and drive to succeed
- I am not afraid of making mistakes or failing at things
- I am now ready to give it all that it takes to succeed

Unfinished Business score out of 10 __

Your Overall Scores:

Area	Score
Self-worth	
Going for it!	
Communication	
Pleasure & fun	
Work confidence	
Looking after yourself	
Growth	
Unfinished Business	
TOTAL	

Put your overall scores in the table above and highlight the areas of your confidence that need the most work.

Jot down below the top 5 activities that you are going to start on immediately. What jumped out at you as a result of completing the above assessment?

1.
2.
3.
4.
5.

So, what was your score?

Use the chart below to see what confidence league you are in!

Points	League
70-80	Premier League
60-69	Division 1
40-59	Division 2
00-39	Division 3

Premier League

You should be writing material not taking tests!

Division 1

Huge potential to jump into the big league. Need to polish your skills in a couple of areas to get promotion.

Division 2

Playing to a good standard but you are underachieving. You have spouts of confidence and then doubts creep in. You need more overall consistency.

Division 3

Well… the only way is up. Sack the current manager and recruit a new one with a proven track record. Make a fresh start from this moment onwards and nothing will stop you.

TAKE ACTION NOW!

You owe it to yourself to have as much happiness in your life as you can. Do something about it today.

Inspiring Books

Dream Big, Aim High. Innovations, creative ideas and execution is possible only if you think positive.

The book advocates all this and covers aspects of growth – emotional, mental & spiritual – to inspire a meaningful life.

Barendra Kumar

ISBN : 9788178061153 Rs.150/-

This is real stuff for real people no lectures, no empty talk, only immensely practical wisdom! That too told in a humorous way by the author who has himself learnt them in the process of surviving some great crises in life, and thus speaks with the authority of personal experience.

ISBN : 9788178061221 Rs.135/-

Dr. L. Prakash

UNICORN BOOKS
F-2/16, Ansari Road, Daryaganj, New Delhi-110002
☎ 23275434, 23262683, 23262783 • Fax: 011-23257790
E-mail: info@unicornbooks.in • Website: www.unicornbooks.in

Best-sellers by Vikas Malkani, a gifted orator

ISBN : 9788178061429 Rs.150/-

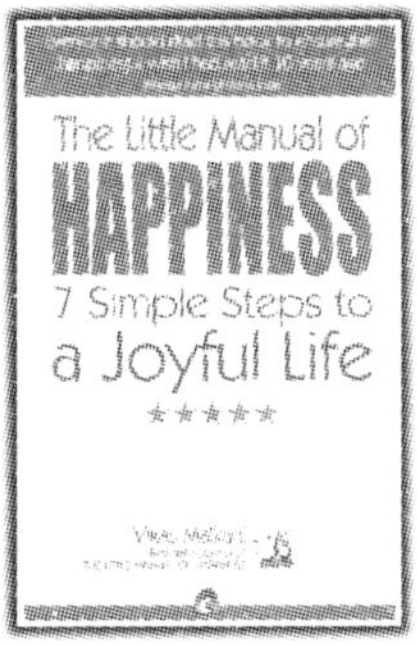

ISBN : 9788178061375 Rs.150/-

Simple steps to success, inner peace and joyful life in this fast moving materialistic world. The ideas expressed in the books drawn from ancient wisdom are simple to understand and easy to apply, to create a life of health, harmony and abundance on all levels.

ISBN : 9788178061382 Rs.150/-

ISBN : 9788178061412 Rs.150/-

UNICORN BOOKS
F-2/16, Ansari Road, Daryaganj, New Delhi-110002
☎ 23275434, 23262683, 23262783 • Fax: 011-23257790
E-mail: info@unicornbooks.in • Website: www.unicornbooks.in